MW01061790

The First Jewish-American Cookbook (1871)

Mrs. Esther Levy

Dover Publications, Inc.
Mineola, New York

Bibliographical Note

This Dover edition, first published in 2004, is an unabridged republication of the work originally published in 1871 by W. S. Turner, Philadelphia, under the title, *Jewish Cookery Book, on Principles of Economy, Adapted for Jewish Housekeepers, with the Addition of Many Useful Medicinal Recipes, and Other Valuable Information, Relative to Housekeeping and Domestic Management*. For the convenience of the reader, a Table of Contents has been added to this edition on page 2.

Library of Congress Cataloging-in-Publication Data

Levy, Esther.
[Jewish cookery book]
The first Jewish-American cookbook (1871) / Mrs. Esther Levy.
p. cm.
Originally published under title: Jewish cookery book. Philadelphia : W.S. Turner, 1871.
Includes index.
ISBN 0-486-43732-9 (pbk.)
1. Cookery, Jewish. I. Title.

TX724.L4 2004
641.5'676—dc22

2004050193

Manufactured in the United States of America
Dover Publications, Inc., 31 East 2nd Street, Mineola, N.Y. 11501

מלאכת הבישול בדרך נכון וכפי מצות דתנו הקדושה

A COOKERY BOOK PROPERLY EXPLAINED, AND IN ACCORDANCE WITH THE RULES OF THE JEWISH RELIGION.

JEWISH COOKERY BOOK,

ON

PRINCIPLES OF ECONOMY,

ADAPTED FOR

JEWISH HOUSEKEEPERS,

WITH THE ADDITION OF MANY USEFUL MEDICINAL RECIPES,

AND

Other Valuable Information,

RELATIVE TO HOUSEKEEPING AND DOMESTIC MANAGEMENT.

BY MRS. ESTHER LEVY,

(Neé Esther Jacobs.)

PHILADELPHIA:

W. S. TURNER, No. 808 CHESTNUT STREET.

1871.

CONTENTS

ERRATA

Page 5, line 14, for "an hour" read "a half-hour."

Page 8, line 3, for "the house must be thoroughly cleaned" read "the house must be found clean."

Page 18, line 10, for "After the fish is well washed" add "and sprinkled with salt one hour before cooking."

Page 28, line 5, for "*Frimsel*" read "*Griebus.*"

Page 30, line 32, *Ox Tail Soup,* for "ushered" read "coshered."

Page 69, line 16, in *Ice Cake,* for "flour" read "sugar."

Page 71, line 19, *Butter Cakes,* for "ground rice" read "ground almonds."

Page 72, line 31, *Ground Rice Cake,* for "cinnamon" read "almonds."

Page 77, line 28, *Macaroons,* for "four ounces of ground almonds" read "one pound of ground almonds."

Page 103, line 5, *German Puffs,* after "quart of milk" add "four ounces of butter."

PREFACE.

As every book appears incomplete without a preface, we will say a few words to the Jewish public. Having undertaken the present work with the view of proving that, without violating the precepts of our religion, a table can be spread, which will satisfy the appetites of the most fastidious. Some have, from ignorance, been led to believe that a repast, to be sumptuous, must unavoidably admit of forbidden food. We do not venture too much when we assert that our writing clearly refutes that false notion. The contents of our Book show how various and how grateful to the taste are the viands of which we may lawfully partake. We submit it to the attention of our sisters in faith. From the days of our mother, Sarah—when her husband bids her "make cakes" for his celestial guests—Jewesses have not disdained attending to culinary matters. Indeed, one of the qualities attributed to the model woman of the book of

Proverbs is, that she "riseth while it is yet night and giveth provision to her household." We of the present age may not be quite so industrious, but we cannot be charged with being dilatory in doing that which contributes to the comfort of our families.

That the ability to cook well, and to present our aliment in different ways, is calculated to preserve the health and to embrace the pleasures of home, cannot possibly be denied. We have labored to further that most desirable object. And if, together with the directions we have given in a material point of view, those also will be heeded which we have offered regarding the observance of some of our practices, we trust that our efforts will redound to the spiritual welfare of our co-religionists, and secure for ourselves their kind approbation.

INTRODUCTION.

The want of a work of this description has long been felt in our domestic circles. I will first endeavor to give some information as to the manner of strictly keeping a Jewish house. We must have on the door posts, the name of the God of Israel, written on parchment, in Hebrew, viz.: two passages from Deuteronomy, in which the unity of God and the reward or punishment attending our actions are taught; the first commencing with the words: "Hear, O Israel;" the second, "and it shall come to pass if you will hearken diligently," etc. We must observe to have the meat (כשר) coshered and porged by a butcher, that is, to take out the veins and sinews, which are prohibited. Then lay the meat in cold water for an hour, afterwards on a perforated board, sprinkling salt on all sides, for about an hour. It must remain there in order to draw out the blood forbidden to our people, after which it must be rinsed under the hydrant, and wiped with a cloth; likewise, all the utensils used for that purpose must be well rinsed.

We must have the Sabbath food prepared on Friday; and it is customary to break off a piece of the dough of two loaves, which are made in commemoration of an ancient offering, and burn it, accompanying the action with a blessing. At sundown the Sabbath lamps must be lighted with a special blessing.

In every rank of life, those deserve the greatest praise who best acquit themselves of the duties which their stations in life require. Indeed, apart from any advantage we may desire, we should try to be equal to the task that nature seems to have imposed on us, in order that we may maintain the dignity of our character as rational beings. It frequently occurs that before impressions of duty are made on the mind, ornamental education commences, and it ever after takes the lead. Thus, what should be only an embellishment, becomes the main business of life. There is no opportunity for attaining a knowledge of family management at school, and during vacation all subjects that might interfere with amusement are avoided. The direction of a table is no inconsiderable branch of a lady's business, as it involves judgment in expenditure, respectability of appearance, the comfort of one's household, and of those who partake of the hospitality thereof.

In carving, some people haggle meat so much as not to be able to help half a dozen persons decently from a large joint or tongue. If the daughters of the family were to take the head of the table, under the direction of their mother, they would fulfil its duties with grace, in the same easy manner as an early practice in other domestic duties gradually fits them for their fulfilment in after years. Habit alone can make good carvers. If a lady has never been accustomed, while single, to think of family management, let her not upon that account fear that she cannot attain it. She may consult others who are more experienced, and acquaint herself with the necessary quantity of the several articles of family expenditure, in proportion to the number it consists of, the proper prices to pay, etc.

When young ladies marry, they continue to employ their own maids in the capacity of housekeepers, who, supposing they are more attached to the interests of their employers than strangers, become very valuable servants. To such, the economical observations in this work will be as useful as those for cooking. It is recommended, however, strictly to observe both, which, in the course of a year or two, will make them familiar with what is requisite. By good hours, especially early breakfast, a family becomes more regular in its habits, and much time is saved. If orders be given soon in the morning, there will be more time to execute them, and servants, by doing their work with ease, will be more equal to it, and fewer of them will be necessary.

Without suspecting any one's honesty, still, as mistakes may have been made unintentionally, it is prudent to weigh meats, sugar, etc., when brought in, and compare with the charge. The butcher should be ordered to send the weight with the meat, and the cook to file the checks, to be examined when the weekly bill shall be delivered.

Much confusion and trouble are saved when there is company, if servants are required to prepare the table and sideboard in a similar manner, daily. All things likely to be wanted should be in readiness. Sugars of different qualities kept broken; currants washed, picked, and kept perfectly dry; spices ground, and kept in very small bottles, closely corked; not more than will be used in four or five weeks. Every article should be kept in its proper place, for much waste may thereby be avoided.

In preparing for the Passover, which generally commences in the middle of spring and lasts eight days, every particle of leaven must be out of the house by ten o'clock of the preceding morning. On the same day, 14th of Nisan, or on the previous eve, the house must be thoroughly cleaned from dirt, and everything be in perfect order.

With what pleasurable emotions a Jewish woman must anticipate the time when she will see everything looking so brilliantly clean, and mostly new. Indeed, we all should be delighted, when we reflect that so much cleanliness is a preparation for becomingly celebrating our wonderful deliverance from bondage.

It is customary, when the synagogue service is over, for the master of the house to sit down to a table prepared with Passover cakes, parsley, chervil, horseradish, a lamb bone, and baked eggs, as well as wine, usually made in this country with raisins. The Passover cakes are placed between napkins. The herbs are placed upon a plate, together with a glass of salt water or vinegar, prepared for Passover, and a mixture made of chopped apples and raisins, and almonds rolled in cinnamon balls ; all of these being symbolical of events of the past, in the history of our people. The humblest Jewish servant must sit at the table during the prayers, which occupy three-quarters of an hour before supper. When ready for this, everything there was on the table, during the reciting of the prayers, must be removed. The supper generally consists of some well-prepared fish, etc. It is not usual to partake of anything roasted on that eve or the next day.

On the day previous we are accustomed to dine on stewed beef, with potatoes, for matzos are not to be eaten until the evening prayers are read, and a blessing said over the unleaven cakes. After Passover, all things used for the occasion, such as crockery or saucepans, and anything that has been used for cooking, during that time, must be thoroughly cleansed, leaving no particle of food on them. They should be put away for the next year in a separate closet, usually kept for that purpose. Sometimes it is necessary to keep out some for the rest of the year, but they must be replaced with new at the returning of that holiday. Be sure to observe that everything is perfectly dry previous to storing it away.

Before using the kitchen tables, they must undergo a thorough scrubbing, and be rinsed with scalding water. It was customary in England to lay them in fuller's earth, which is not so well known here, and is more expensive; so it would be advisable to have coarse cloths tacked on instead. The cisterns must be cleaned, and a piece of flannel put on the nozzle of the hydrant; at all times such a thing might be applied, as there are a number of insects that will appear when the water is drawn, too small to be perceived by the naked eye. Chopping boards must either be new or those that were used for a former Passover. It is necessary to be very particular, so that there shall not be the slightest part of leaven in our habitations.

ARRANGEMENT OF THE TABLE.

For Breakfast.

The table should be laid with a clean white cloth, the cups and saucers at one end, if for tea; at both ends, if for tea and coffee. The tea pot and coffee pot occupy the space between in front, and the urn at the back; the slop basin and milk jug should be placed to the left, and the cream and hot milk jugs to the right; the remainder of the table should be occupied in the centre by the various dishes, while at the sides must be ranged a large plate for eggs, fish, etc., and a small plate for toast and rolls, etc., with a knife and fork for each person; the butter knives to the right of the dishes; and spoons in front of the hot dishes with gravy; and individual salt-cellars for each person; the cruets should be placed in the centre of the table.

For Luncheon.

Bring in a tray, with let-down sides, on which has been previously arranged a tray cloth, and letting down the sides and spreading the cloth upon the dining-room table to distribute the things as required. The sides of the table are occupied by the requisites for each guest: two plates, a large and small knife and fork and dessert spoon, a folded napkin, and the bread under it, which are to be arranged in front of the place of each guest.

The dishes generally served for lunch are the remains of cold meat, fish, or poultry, neatly trimmed or garnished, or sweetmeats, or fruit, or plainly cooked cutlets, chops, or steaks, or in fact anything does for lunch; cheese or eggs, or bread and butter and pickles. A good housekeeper will always have something in the house for lunch. Ale, porter, home-made wines, or sherry is generally drank.

For Dinner.

The table should be well polished and covered with a green baize cloth, over which a fine damask one should be spread. If the white cloth is to be kept on after dinner, (some persons use an entire upper cloth, to prevent gravy stains or accidents, which is removed after dinner,) it does not require the tedious brushing the cloth.

When the cloth has been spread, place finger glasses, with the tumblers belonging to and placed over them, between every four persons; a salt-cellar between every third person, and a large and small knife, fork, and spoon to each guest, with two wine glasses, a champagne glass, and tumbler to the right of each person, and the bread placed on or under folded napkins, between the knives and forks and spoons. At grand entertainments, or public dinners, the name and rank of each guest should be neatly written on a card, in front of napkin, to prevent confusion and jealousy.

The centre ornament, usually a candelabrum, or epergne, or a vase of real or artificial flowers, must be set on the table, and the mats for the various dishes arranged. The wine coolers, or ornamental vases, are placed between the centre-piece and the top and bottom dishes, with the wines in the original bottles, loosely corked, The spoons for assisting the various dishes, asparagus tongs, fish knife and fork or slice, are placed in front of the dishes to which they belong, and a knife rests opposite to those who carve, with a bill of fare, and a pile of soup plates before those that have to assist with the soup.

Particular attention must be paid to the cleanliness of the plate and glasses, so that they have a bright polish. Nothing looks so bad as dirty, greasy looking silver and glasses. Glass should be rubbed with a fine wash leather, dipped in a solution of whiting and stone blue, and then dried and polished with an old silk handkerchief. Plates and dishes must be hot. Bread should be cut in pieces about an inch thick, or pastry rolls should be used. Lights, either at or after dinner, should be subdued and above the guests, if possible, so as to be shed upon the table without intercepting the view. Sauces, either bottled or sweet, or both, vegetables and sliced cucumbers, or glazed onions, for fall goose, should always be placed on the sideboard. A plate for removing the soiled plates is usually placed under the sideboard or some other convenient part of the room, and two knife trays, covered with napkins, are placed upon a tray. These are used for removing the soiled knives and forks, and the soiled silver. There should always be a corkscrew ready, and funnel with strainer, and brad-awl to break the wire of the champagne bottles, and the other to strain port wine, if required for dinner.

To place Dishes on the Table.

Each servant should be provided at large dinner parties with a bill of fare, and instructed at small ones where the dishes are to be placed. No two dishes resembling each other should be placed near the same part of the table. Soup should always be placed at the head of the table, if there are two, top and bottom, if four, top and bottom and two sides, with fish alternating. Fish should be placed at the head of the table; if two sorts, have fried at the bottom of the table, and boiled at the top. If there are four sorts, arrange the same as the soup. Fish is generally served on a napkin, the corners of which are either turned in or thrown over the fish.

The first course generally consists of soups and fish, which are removed for the roasts, stews, etc., of the second course.

The second course, when there are three, consists of roasts and stews, for the top and bottom. Turkeys or fowls and smoked beef, garnished tongue or fricandeau, for the side, with small made dishes for corners, served in covered dishes, as curries, ragouts, fricassees, stews, etc.

When there are two roasts, one should be white and the other brown. Removes are generally upon large dishes, for, as they supply the place of the fish and soups, they constitute the principal part of the dinner.

Entrées, or made dishes, require great care in placing them upon the table or the gravy runs over and soils the dish. They are served with a wall of mashed potatoes, to keep them in their proper place, or rice, or other vegetables. They should be served as hot as possible.

The third course consists of confectionery, delicate vegetables dressed in the French style, puddings, creams, jellies, etc. When there are only two courses, the first generally consists of soups and fish, removed by boiled poultry, smoked beef tongue, stews, roasts, ragouts, curries, or made dishes generally, with vegetables. The second consists of roasted poultry at the top and bottom of the table, with dressed vegetables, macaroni, jellies, water ices, creams, preserves, fruit, pastry, and general confectionery, salads, etc. It is generally contrived to give as great a variety as possible, in their dinners. Thus, a jelly, a compote, an ornamental cake, a dish of preserved fruit, fritters, a blanc-mange, a pudding, celery, etc.

The side and corner dishes, usually put on for dessert, consists of compotes in glass dishes, frosted fruit, served on lace-paper in small glass dishes; preserved and dried fruit in small glass dishes; biscuits, fresh fruit, served in dishes, surrounded with leaves or moss, olives, or wafer biscuits, brandy scrolls in the centre. Dishes may consist of a Savoy, or an ornamental cake, on an elevated stand; a group of wax fruit, surrounded with moss; a melon, or pineapple, grapes, or a vase of flowers.

JEWISH COOKERY.

FISH.

Observations on Dressing Fish.

Be careful to scrape off the scales and wash the inside perfectly clean. Do not allow the fish to remain too long in the water, as it will spoil its flavor. When quite clean, if to be fried, sprinkle lightly with salt a half hour before cooking; if to be boiled, a little vinegar should be put in the water, with a handful of salt, to keep it firm. Those who understand how to purchase fish, may, by taking more at a time than they want for one day, often get it cheap; such kinds as will pot or pickle, or keep by being sprinkled with salt and hung up, or by being dried, will serve for stewing the next day, may then be bought with advantage.

TO BOIL FISH.—All large fish, such as rock, salmon or halibut, with the skin whole, must be wrapped in a cloth with twine tied around it, and boiled in cold water; it must not be covered with more than two inches of water; put in a good handful of salt, when the water begins to boil skim it well, and remove it to one side and let it boil gently till done; the fish will separate from the bone when it is cooked, if it falls from the bone it is over-cooked; the exact time for boiling must be according to the size of the fish; Salmon will take longer. Take the cloth and twine off the fish carefully, and turn it upon a dish with a napkin; serve with drawn butter or egg sauce. If there is a strainer to your saucepan, there is no need for a cloth. In boiling salt cod fish, previously soak it for a day, change the water until fresh, then boil it gently, take it apart with a fork, thicken it with milk, butter and flour, dish it up hot and eat it with sauce.

TO FRY FISH.—If fish is to be fried or broiled, it must be wrapped in a nice soft cloth, after it is well washed. When perfectly dry, place some sweet olive oil in a frying pan, and be sure to observe that it must boil; and put a small piece of stale bread in the pan before the fish is put in, beat up some eggs, to three pound of fish two eggs will suffice, and a quarter of a pint of oil and some flour in a plate, then dip the fish in the flour smoothly and then in the egg, then put it into the boiling oil and let it fry quickly on one side, and turn it over to cook on the other side, and then turn it a third time on the other side to finish; take it out carefully with a fish slice, and place it on a dish to remain two or three hours; then change your fish on another dish for the table, to be garnished with fresh parsley around the dish. The same oil, with a little fresh added will do again. Butter gives a bad color and not so good a flavor. For those who will allow the expense oil is by far the cheapest, as it takes the smallest amount, used with care.

TO BROIL FISH.—Broiled fish must be seasoned with pepper and salt; then floured and put on a gridiron that is very clean, which, when hot, must be greased with a little butter, if for breakfast, or with oil for dinner, to prevent the fish from sticking. It must be broiled on a very clear fire, that it may not taste smoky, and not too near that it may be scorched. If the fire is smoky, throw some salt on it, and it will get clear.

ENTREE FISH.—Chop fine four white fish, and rub them through a fine wire sieve, put this in a mortar with a quarter of a pound of fresh butter, an equal quantity of bread crumbs, pound these until well mixed; season with pepper, salt and nutmeg, add three yolks of eggs, beating all for five minutes, then add two whole eggs, mix all well together; then take up in a basin, add a spoonful of cream and the juice of a lemon, next shake some flour on a clean board or slab, divide the ingredients with a spoon into twelve equal parts, roll these, with the hand dipped into flour, in small oval shapes, dip in beaten eggs and place them in a frying pan with butter; when fried sufficiently dish them up close together, fill the centre with cooked mushrooms or truffles, pour round some sauce of lemon and egg, and the gravy made from the bones of the fish; any kind of good fish can be cooked the same way.

LEMON STEWED FISH.—Have washed and scraped clean the nape or head and shoulders of halibut, or any good firm fish; cut it up small and lay it in a stewpan, with one pint of water and three or four good sized onions, fried in oil a light brown; put them on top of the fish, with some cayenne pepper, a little ground mace, and a teaspoonful of ground ginger, with two tablespoonfuls of salt; let it all stew gently until it is done; if there should be too much gravy on it before adding the sauce, take it off; prepare two eggs and six good sized lemons, squeezed and strained; then take some of the gravy from the fish, while it is boiling, add it to the lemon, with the two eggs well beaten, and a tablespoonful of flour; mix smoothly with some chopped parsley; when all is well mixed, put it to the fish, shake it gently for five minutes while it is boiling, taking care not to let it burn; when it is sufficiently cooked, let it stand for an hour, and dish it up. Garnish with slices of lemon and parsley. To be eaten cold. Fish balls are made with it, as in recipe for fish balls.

A GOOD BROWN STEWED FISH.—Take either some carp or shad, and place it in your stewpan, with a pint of vinegar, a quarter of a pound of dark molasses and a couple of sliced onions, some ginger, a tablespoonful of salt, pepper, mace, allspice, nutmeg and a little piece of cinnamon, and let them stew together until done; then mix some gingerbread with the gravy and a few raspings of bread, and pour on the fish, and let all boil up together for a few minutes, and dish up. To be eaten cold.

POLISH STEWED FISH.—Take some pike, after being well washed, and place it in a stewpan, with a pint of water, a small piece of butter, a little ginger, pepper, salt and chopped parsley, and let them stew well; when done, roll some butter in flour and add to the fish; let all boil together for a few minutes, and dish up. To be eaten either cold or hot.

TO MAKE STEWED FISH-BALLS.—Take some fish, clear from the bone, and chop it up with some cod liver and bread crumbs, grate with parsley, ginger, pepper, a little mace and salt, and a beaten egg; mix all the ingredients together and stew with your fish, not too stiff, with bread crumbs; be sure to beat your egg first, as it will bind the articles together.

BAKED HADDOCK.—Take a haddock of five or six pounds, after it has been well cleaned, and lay it in a baking dish, with a half pint of water, a quarter of a pound of butter, broken into small pieces, and some pepper, ginger and salt; sprinkle flour and rasped bread crust over the fish; a stuffing of bread crumbs, chopped parsley, thyme, marjoram, pepper and salt, and eggs beaten up, all mixed together, with a small piece of butter, to be put inside the fish, and with some potatoes cut in thin slices around it. Bake in a good oven for one hour and a half.

SALMON, WITH PEAS.—Take three or four pounds of salmon, cut into slices two inches thick, and place in a saucepan with some young green peas, in sufficient water to cover them, with a good sized piece of butter, pepper, salt and ginger, and let them stew for three-quarters of an hour; when done mix a little flour and milk and pour over them, and let it boil up, shaking the saucepan carefully for two or three minutes.

TO POT SALMON.—Take a large piece, scale and wipe, but do not wash it; salt it very well, and let it lie till the salt is melted and drained from it, then season with beaten mace, cloves and whole pepper; lay in a few bay leaves; put it close into a pan; cover it over with butter, and bake it: when well done drain it from the gravy; put it into pots to keep. When cold, cover it with clarified butter; in this manner any kind of firm fish may be done.

TO POT SHAD, HERRING OR OTHER FISH.—Let the fish be well scraped and washed, then lay it for three or four hours in salt; take a good sized jar, and cut the fish in pieces to fit; season it with salt, pepper, cinnamon, cloves, mace and ginger; put in the jar a layer of fish, one of spices, strewed over smoothly, then sprinkle a little flour over, and pieces of good butter, and so on alternately until the jar is full; pack it down tightly, then fill the jar with vinegar and a little water, cover the jar with a crust made of flour and water, press close to the jar that the steam may not escape; bake it in a gentle oven for five or six hours. Do not remove it from the jar until it is cold. Slice it thin and serve with lemon sauce.

TO PICKLE SALMON.—Split the salmon and divide it into good sized pieces, lay it in the saucepan, with as much water as will cover it; to three quarts of water put a pint of vinegar, a handful of salt, twelve bay leaves, six blades of whole mace and a quarter of an ounce of black pepper; when the salmon is boiled enough, drain it and put it on a clean cloth, then put more salmon into the saucepan and pour the liquor upon it, and so on till done. After this, if the pickle be not strongly flavored with the vinegar and salt, add more, and boil it quickly three-quarters of an hour. When all is cold, pack the fish in something deep, and let there be enough of pickle to cover and preserve it from the air; the liquor must be drained from the fish, and occasionally boiled and skimmed.

SAUCE FOR BOILED FISH.—Make the sauce in this way: Take one cup of butter, rub in it a tablespoonful of flour, a little salt and pepper, then add to it a pint of cold water, boil it gently, stirring it all the time; you can add more butter if you wish it richer; also chopped parsley. For egg sauce, add to the above hard boiled eggs, chopped fine.

CAPER SAUCE FOR FISH.—Chop some capers quite small, some melted butter, and a little of the liquor off the fish, and three anchovies chopped fine and a little of the essence; mix all together with salt, pepper and ginger, and boil all smoothly.

BREAD SAUCE FOR FISH.—Grate some light bread, to which add some pepper, two onions, a little salt, and boil the milk to cover it; let it simmer gently until the bread soaks up the milk; then add some cream, make it very hot, strained if preferred, and pour it over the fish.

BUTTER SAUCE FOR BROILED FISH—Take a good sized piece of butter, roll it up with one ounce of flour, pour over it a quarter pint of boiling milk, stir it smoothly and boil for a few minutes, add a little salt and chopped parsley to make it rich; when boiled break up an egg in the sauce tureen, and pour it over the boiling sauce, stirring all the time.

A GOOD BUTTER SAUCE FOR BOILED FISH.—Take a small sized piece of butter and roll it up in one ounce of flour until fine, clear of lumps; have some milk boiling, then take a few spoonfuls of it and add it to the butter, so on until it is all smooth, and boil it up with a little salt, ginger and chopped parsley.

BURNT BUTTER SAUCE.—Fry some butter, and when it begins to smoke throw into it some chopped parsley; when quite done, add pepper, salt and a teaspoonful of vinegar.

ANCHOVY SAUCE.—Take two tablespoonfuls of essence of anchovies, add to it some good butter sauce and a little lemon juice.

FENNEL SAUCE FOR BOILED MACKEREL.—Chop very fine a bunch of green fennel, add to it some good butter sauce, let it look nice and green, a little cayenne and a tablespoonful of lemon juice.

MUSTARD SAUCE.—A tablespoonful of mustard, and a tablespoonful of vinegar can be added to some good butter sauce. If made in butter, same recipe.

EGG SAUCE No. 1.—Boil two or three eggs hard, when they are cold cut them up in small square pieces, and put them in some good butter, seasoned with salt and pepper.

EGG SAUCE No. 2.—Take four hard boiled eggs, cut the whites into small pieces and put them into a stew-pan, then rub the yolks through an iron sieve, keep them separate until the sauce is prepared, pour some good butter sauce over the whites, add a teaspoonful of English mustard, pepper, salt and lemon juice; before dishing up the sauce warm it, then mix the yolks of the eggs, which will look like vermicelli.

FISH SALAD.—Two pounds of cold boiled halibut or rock fish, or any hard fish, cut it up small, and prepare the same sauce as herb; and chop up some anchovies fine with anchovy sauce, and pour all on the fish in a salad bowl; if onions are liked they may be used with some chopped parsley. Garnish the dish with some good dutch herring, previously soaked for an hour, and horse radish scraped fine. Place hard boiled eggs cut in slices around the bowl in fanciful style.

FISH CAKE.—Take the bones from fish of any kind; put the head and bones into a stewpan with a pint of water, a little salt, pepper, an onion and some sweet herbs to stew for gravy. Chop the fish up and mix it well with some crumbs of bread and cold potatoes, equal parts, a little parsley and seasoning. Make into a cake, with the white of an egg or a little butter or milk, egg it over and cover with bread crumbs, then fry a light brown. Pour the gravy over and stew gently for fifteen minutes, stirring it carefully twice or thrice; serve hot and garnish with slices of lemon or parsley.

SALAMAGUNDY.—For this purpose, chop separately the white part of cold chicken or veal, yolks of eggs, boiled hard, the whites of eggs, parsley, half a dozen anchovies, red beet root, pickled cabbage, smoked beef, grated tongue, or anything well flavored and of a good color, a little onion, if desirable; put a saucer into a small dish, then make rows round it, wide at the bottom and growing smaller towards the top; choose such of the ingredients for each row as will most vary the colors. At the top a little sprig of parsley may be stuck in, or without anything in the dish, the salamagundy may be laid in rows, or put into it the half of the whites of the eggs, which may be made to stand upright, by cutting off a bit at the round end.

SOUPS.

SPRING SOUP.—Take a shin of beef, a piece of mutton, and two pounds of beef. Cut, in the shape of dice, some vegetables, such as cabbage, lettuce, tarragon, chevril, asparagus, young peas, and cucumbers. Cut the asparagus an inch long; add a few French beans, and a cauliflower, cut small. Season with a little cayenne pepper, salt, ginger, mace, and a little nutmeg.

BARLEY SOUP.—Take four or five pounds of good boiling beef, and place it in a saucepan, with three quarts of cold water; have ready, boiled well, half a pound of good pearl barley, add it to the soup. Season with a little ginger, salt, pepper, nutmeg, and chopped vegetables.

Rice soup may be made in the same way.

MOCK TURTLE SOUP.—Get a calf's head, with the skin on, but cleaned from the hair. Half boil it; take all the meat off in square pieces; break the bones of the head, and boil them in some good veal and beef broth to make it richer; fry some shalot and flour enough to thicken the gravy; stir this into the browning, and give it one or two boils; skim it carefully, and then put in the head; put in a pint of Madeira wine, and simmer till the meat is quite tender. About ten minutes before you serve, put in some chives, parsley, cayenne pepper, and salt to your taste; also, two squeezes of lemon, two spoonfuls of mushroom ketchup, and one of soy. Pour the soup into the tureen. Force-meat balls and yolks of hard boiled eggs. There are various ways of making this soup, but I choose this as preferable.

TO MAKE A GOOD FRIMSEL (OR NOODLE) SOUP.—Take a piece of thick brisket, about five or six pounds for a large family, and a knuckle of veal, and put in a saucepan, with water sufficient to cover the meat, about, for that quantity of meat, two and a half quarts of water, with an onion, celery, parsley, a little pepper, ginger, and mace. Some persons use saffron, dried and pounded, just a small pinch; boil for three hours. Take out the meat, and strain the soup; then return it to the saucepan. Have ready some vermicelli or frimsels, and let the soup come up to a boil; then throw in, lightly, the frimsels, and boil for ten minutes. Two ounces of flour and one egg, with a pinch of salt and ginger, will make sufficient frimsels; or two eggs and a quarter of a pound of flour, for a large family.

NOODLE SOUP.—Prepare soup, as in directions for soups. Take two eggs and beat them well with a little salt. Stir the eggs into a pound of flour, until you make as stiff paste as you can; roll out into two or three cakes, as thin as possible; the thinner the better. Flour the board and pin while rolling. After one piece is rolled lay it on a clean place to dry, and so on, till all the pieces are rolled out. Half an hour will suffice to dry them. After this, fold each cake in one long roll, and cut with a very sharp knife in shreds as fine as possible. Shake these separately aud let them dry a little. After your soup is ready and strained, drop the noodles in very lightly, and boil for fifteen minutes. If you have more than is required at the same time, they can be put away in a cool, dry place for a few days; but they are always best fresh made.

JULIENNE SOUP.—Take some carrots and turnips, and cut them ribbon-like; a few heads of celery, some leeks and onions, and cut them round. Boil them till tender; then put them in some clear gravy soup; brown thickening. In summer you may add green peas, asparagus tops, French beans or some grated carrots.

MUTTON SOUP.—Take a scrag of mutton, put it in a saucepan, with a small piece of beef, and three quarts of water, some pepper, ginger, a little mace and salt. Let it come to a boil, and then skim it quite clean, and put in some turnips and onions, and let all boil together until tender. Take out the turnips and mash them with some pepper and salt, and add to the soup some flour to thicken.

POTATO SOUP.—Take a piece of boiling meat, with some scraps of mutton; cut up some potatoes in slices, and four or five onions, and let them all stew together, with two quarts of water. Add pepper, salt, and ginger.

MULLIGATAWNEY SOUP.—Divide a calf's head, well cleaned, and a cow's heel, and put them in a saucepan, with two quarts of water. Let them boil till tender. When cool, cut the meat from the bones in slices, and fry them in melted fat, or drippings from the roast meat, or fat skimmed from soup. Stew the bones of the head and heel for four hours. Strain, and let it get cold, then skim off the fat. When done, cut four or five onions in slices, and fry them brown; then add two tablespoonfuls of curry powder, half a teaspoonful of cayenne pepper, a tablespoonful of salt, a teaspoonful of turmeric; (it is an improvement that can be dispensed with;) add all these ingredients to the soup. Boil gently for two hours, then add one tablespoonful of Harvey's sauce, and dish up hot.

OLD PEA SOUP.—Take a quart of split peas, soak over night, and put them in a saucepan with the same water, after having washed and picked them clean, with some pepper, ginger, mace, and salt, a bone of cold roast beef, or a piece of shin, or boiling meat, and boil until all is tender. Fry some stale bread, and cut up in small shapes, and some mint, dried and rubbed fine.

A GOOD WAY TO MAKE POTATO SOUP.—Take stock of soup, a pound, sliced thin; boil a half pound of potatoes, a pint of green peas, an onion, and three ounces of rice in the stock. Strain it through a colander; then pulp the peas to it, and turn it into the saucepan again with two heads of celery, sliced. Stew it tender, and add pepper and salt; served up with fried bread.

VEGETABLE SOUP.—Take half a pound of butter, and put it into a stewpan; then cut up some lettuce, a sprig or two of mint, two or three onions, some pepper, salt, a pint and a half of young peas, a little parsley, and two or three young turnips. Let them stew in their own liquor, near a gentle fire, half an hour; then pour two quarts of water to the vegetables, and stew them two hours. Take a little flour and make it smooth in a cup of water. Boil it with the rest fifteen or twenty minutes and serve it.

OX-TAIL SOUP.—Cut up two tails into joints, after they have been ushered, or cleansed from the blood.

Then take some clear stock, and put them in a saucepan and let them boil until tender. Skim off all the grease; then add some carrots, cut in pieces, and some very small onions. Do not over-stew it. Season with cayenne pepper, whole ginger, whole mace, salt, nutmeg, a tablespoonful of Harvey's sauce, and dish up with the tails in the tureen.

SAGO SOUP.—Take a piece of brisket, of three or four pounds, and put it in a saucepan, with two quarts of water, an onion fried in fat, a few sweet herbs and parsley, a teaspoonful of black pepper, a little cloves, mace, allspice, and some salt. Then take out the meat, and strain the soup. Return the soup to a clean pan, and thicken it with a quarter of a pound of sago. Let it boil tender. Dish up with sippets of toast or fried bread.

NICE BUTTER SOUP, (*for the (nine tag) nine days of lamentation.*)—Take a peck of nice young peas, and place then in a saucepan, with two quarts of cold water to cover them. Cut up some young turnips, carrots, parsley, onions, and cauliflower into very small pieces, with some pepper, ginger, mace, and a good lump of butter; let them all simmer together. When done, put in some drop dumpling, made in this way: take four eggs, well beaten, one pound of flour, one pint of milk, and thicken as a batter, with some salt, ginger, and parsley, chopped, and drop them in the soup. Boil the dumplings gently for a quarter of an hour.

OCHRE SOUP.—Prepare a chicken or piece of nice brisket, as that always makes most delicious soup, with about two dozen ochres, six tomatoes, six onions, thyme, parsley, salt and red pepper; set them all in a saucepan, with two quarts of cold water; the ochre can be powdered, and thicken the soup with it; celery can be used if preferred.

OCHRE SOUP, OR GUMBO.—Ochre soup is much used in the South. Ochre should be grown in a warm, rich soil, and picked for use when in its soft, milky state, like corn; it colors the soup, if allowed to grow firm before picking. Have a good soup prepared, with chicken, and stir into it the ochre, which thickens it and forms into a jelly, which is very pleasant; slice a chicken that has been cooked into shreds, add to it slices of salt beef cut into small pieces, put them over the fire; add chopped celery, onions, spices, if liked, and thicken with the ochre; stew for three hours.

MATZO CLEIS SOUP. (*For Passover.*)—Set your soup as in other soups. Soak two matzos, or crackers, in cold water, and then fry two or three chopped onions in some suet fat; squeeze and strain the soaked matzos, beat it up with three or four eggs and the meal; add the onions and chopped parsley and mix all together with some pepper, salt, ginger, and nutmeg grated, and make it into round balls, pretty stiff, and boil for ten minutes, not more, or they will break.

DROP DUMPLINGS FOR SOUP.—Two eggs, well beaten, with half a pound of flour, and sufficient water to make a middling thick batter, a little salt and chopped parsley; drop dumplings in the soup, ten minutes before dishing. Cook over a gentle fire.

TO KEEP SOUP FROM SOURING.—Do not use any metal dishes to keep soup in. Pans used for this purpose should be scalded every day, and changed. In preparing soup, if too weak, do not cover the pot in boiling.

A PEPPER POT.—In a pint and a half of water put such vegetables as you wish. In summer, peas, lettuce, spinach and two or three onions. In winter, carrots, turnips, onions and celery. Cut them very small and stew them with a couple of pounds of mutton and a piece of nice beef; season with salt and cayenne, and a few small suet dumplings boiled in it. Instead of mutton, you may use chicken. Pepper pot may be made of various things. A small quantity of rice and a good spoonful of cayenne pepper can be boiled with the whole.

FORCEMEAT FOR SOUPS.—Take some cold meat, cut it in small pieces, and season; make a paste of egg and flour, see frimsels; cut the paste in small pieces, and put the forcemeat in; then fold them in the shape of three-cornered hats, and place in the soup; boil for ten minutes.

MEATS.

How to Choose Good Meat when you Buy.

If the flesh of oxen and beef is young it will have a fine, smooth, open grain; be of good red, and look tender. The fat should look white, not yellow, for when that is of a deep color the meat is seldom good, Beef fed on oil cakes is generally of a yellowish cast, and the flesh is flabby. The grain of cow meat is closer, and the fat whiter than that of ox beef, but the lean is not so bright a red. The grain of bull beef is closer still, the fat is hard and skinny, the lean is of a deep red, and has a stronger scent. Ox beef is the reverse. Ox beef is the richest and largest; but in small families, and to some tastes, heifer beef is better, if finely fed. In old meat there is a streak of horn in the ribs of the beef; the harder this is the older the beef, and the flesh is not so finely flavored.

Veal.—The flesh of a bull-calf is generally firmer but not so white. The fillet of the cow-calf is generally preferred for the udder. The whitest flesh is not the most juicy, having been made so by frequent bleeding, and having had whiting to lick. Choose the meat of which the kidney is well covered with white, thick fat. If the blood vein in the shoulder looks blue, or of a bright red, it is newly killed, but any other color shows it is stale. The other parts should be dry and white; if clammy, or spotted, the meat is stale and bad. The kidney turns first in the loin, and the suet will not then be firm.

Mutton.—Choose this by the firmness of its grain, good color, and firm, white fat. It is not the better for being young. If of a good breed, and well fed, it is better for age, but this only holds with wether mutton. The flesh of the ewe is paler, and the grain finer. Ram mutton is of a very strong flavor; the flesh is of a deep red, and the fat is spongy.

Lamb.—Observe the neck of a forequarter; if the vein is bluish, it is fresh. If it has a green or yellow cast, it is stale. In the hindquarter, if there is a faint smell under the kidneys, and the knuckle is limp, the meat is stale. If the eyes are sunk, the head is not fresh. Grass lamb comes into season in April or May, and continues until August. House lamb may be had in large towns almost all the year, but it is in highest perfection in December and January.

Meat and Vegetables that the frost has touched should be soaked in cold water some time before using; by putting them in hot water, or to the fire, till thawed, makes it impossible for any heat to dress them properly afterwards. If the weather permits, meat eats much better for being hung up for two or three days before it is salted.

Roast beef bones, or any hard pieces cut from the meat, will make excellent pea soup. It should be boiled the day before, as the fat can be better skimmed off. The best way to keep meat, when it is not salted, is to put some pieces of charcoal over it. Wash all meat before using, by placing it in a pan of cold water for half an hour, and take it out and sprinkle salt over it as the dew falls, and let it lay for one hour on a perforated board, and then rinse it under the hydrant. Be sure, before laying it in water, to take out all the veins and sinews, which are unfit to eat. If you wish to roast it, take a nice clean cloth and wipe it dry; dredge some flour outside the meat, and a little salt and pepper, if agreeable; some persons do not like pepper outside of meat. If for boiling, put it in a well-floured cloth, and it will boil white. Be sure to observe that the saucepan is quite clean. The moment it boils, skim it well several times; the more it is skimmed the clearer it will be. Always put the meat in cold water to boil; let it boil gently or it will be hard; be sure and give it sufficient time to boil, as it cannot be hurried. If the steam is kept in, the water will not lessen; therefore, when you wish it to boil away, take off the cover of the soup pot. The time of roasting or boiling must be regulated by the size of a joint and the strength of the fire, the nearness of the meat to it, and in boiling, the regular slow progress it makes. Weigh the meat, and allow for all solid joints a quarter of an hour for every pound, and from ten to twenty minutes over, accordingly as the family like it done.

Veal must be well done, so must lamb and all young meats. In roasting meat, it is best to baste it often, and put a little water in the baking pan, and when nearly done dredge it with flour to make it look rich and frosty. To keep meat hot, it is best to take it up when done; set the dish over a pan of boiling water, and put a deep cover over it, so as not to touch the meat; then throw a cloth over it, this way will not dry up the gravy. Before salting the meat, particularly in the summer, be careful to take out the kernels that are in the fat.

TO SALT BEEF FOR EATING IMMEDIATELY.—Take a piece of four or five pounds, salt it thickly just before you put it in the saucepan; take a coarse cloth, flour it well, put the meat in and fold it up closely, put it into a pot of boiling water, and boil it as long as you would any other salt beef of the same size, and it will be as salt as if done four or five days.

BEEF A-LA-MODE.—Take a piece of nice fat beef. Cut up some smoked beef. Let each piece be near an inch thick, dip them in vinegar, and then into a seasoning, ready prepared, of salt, black pepper, allspice, and cloves, all in fine powder, with parsley, thyme, savory, and marjoram, shred as small as possible, and well mixed. With a sharp knife, make deep holes to insert pieces of fat, called larding, into it; then rub the beef over with the above seasoning, and bind it up tight with tape. Set it in a well-tinned pot, over the stove. Add three or four onions, fried brown, to the beef, with two or three carrots, one turnip, a head or two of celery, and a small quantity of water. Let it simmer gently ten or twelve hours, or till extremely tender. Put the gravy into a pan, remove the fat, and keep the beef covered; then put them together, and add a glass of port wine. Take off the tape, and serve with the vegetables; or you may strain them off, and send them up, cut into dice for garnish. A teacupful of vinegar should be stewed with the beef.

TO COOK A STEAK.—Be careful to have a clear fire and put the gridiron on, or let it get hot; then put the steak on, not too close to the fire; do not prick the meat, but stick your fork in the fat part to turn it; turn it two or three times; season with pepper and salt. Put on the top a piece of melted fat; it will make a good gravy. Serve hot.

Veal cutlets or mutton chops may be broiled the same way.

TO COLLAR BEEF.—Take the thin end of the flank of a fine, tender piece of beef. Lay it in a dish with salt and saltpetre. Turn and rub it every day for a week, and keep it cool. Then take out every bone and gristle; remove the skin of the inside part, and cover it thick with the following seasoning, cut small: a large handful of parsley, some thyme, marjoram, pepper, salt, allspice, and nutmeg. Roll the meat up as tight as possible, and bind it; then boil it gently for seven or eight hours. A cloth must be put round before the tape. Put the beef under a good weight while hot, without undoing it; the shape will then be oval.

PRESSED BEEF.—Take a piece of brisket of eight pounds, cosher it and bone it; roll it tightly in a cloth, with some marjoram, parsley, thyme, cayenne pepper, salt, and nutmeg; then tie it tightly and put it into the brine for two weeks; then take it out and boil it in a saucepan for four hours; let it cool off in its own liquor until next day, when it will jelly; press it down with a heavy weight. To be eaten cold.

A GOOD BROWN STEW OF BEEF.—Take a piece of beef, about three pounds, and one pound of good veal. Cut it into small pieces, and fry with some onions, quite brown. Put all in a saucepan with a quart of water, and stew till tender; add some pepper, salt, ginger, mace, onions, and a spoonfull of mushroom, ketchup, thickened with a little browned flour. Some persons think it good with a tablespoonful of vinegar. Serve up with forcemeat balls.

TO SMOKE MEAT.—After it has been in pickle for sixteen days, drain it out, and send it to be smoked, or place it over a barrel, containing a pan of ignited saw-dust, for some hours every day, until nicely browned.

TO PICKLE MEAT.—After it it (כשר) cosher, rub it in salt. Make a pickle of salt, strong enough for an egg to swim on top of the water; add some saltpetre, a little bay salt, and coarse brown sugar. Boil all together, and skim well; then let it cool; after which set the meat in your tub with the pickle, and keep it pressed down for one or two weeks.

TO COOK A TONGUE.—A tongue that has been dried will take from three to four hours' gentle boiling, after it has been soaked; a pickled tongue from two to three hours, or more, if very large. You can tell when it is done by trying it with a fork.

SOUR TONGUE.—Take a fresh tongue, porge and (כשר) cosher it, put it in a stewpan, with a pint and a half of water; season it with whole cloves, cayenne pepper, two onions, cut fine, and salt, a teaspoonful of allspice, and a little grated nutmeg; let it stew quickly for three hours, till tender; ten minutes before dishing it up, thicken with a table spoonful of brown flour, a gill of vinegar, and one teaspoonful of brown sugar.

TO STEW VEAL.—(A knuckle, with one pound of beef.) Stew it with a short gravy, and some onions, parsley, a little marjoram, pepper, salt, ginger, mace, and a little nutmeg, until tender. Then take a pound of tender beef, and chop small with some onions, (reished,) fried in a little fat, and chop them with the meat, quite small, and add some ginger, pepper, a little ground mace, and salt. Mix all together, with some stale bread crumbs and an egg beaten up; roll them in little balls, and add them to the stew. For brown stew, fry the meat and balls as if for a white stew. Add the juice of two lemons and one egg, with some of the gravy. Before dishing up the brown stew, add a little walnut ketchup, and a tablespoonful of vinegar, thickened with a tablespoonful of flour. Ten minutes before dishing up, put some fried bread, cut into shapes, around the dish, to send to the table.

TO ROAST A FILLET OF VEAL, No. 1.—Take a fillet of veal, fit for roasting. Chop some sage and onions small, with some bread crumbs, pepper, and salt. Mix together, and stuff it in the meat. Season it with ginger, salt, and flour, and roast a nice brown. Baste it well with beef drippings.

TO ROAST VEAL, No. 2.—Take some bread crumbs, with some marjoram, thyme, parsley, pepper, ginger, nutmeg, salt, and chopped suet. Mix them all together with an egg, and stuff the meat. Roast in the same manner as No. 1; be sure to baste well.

ROAST MUTTON.—(A shoulder.)—Take some flour, ginger, and salt, and rub it over the mutton. Bake it with some sage, onions, and split potatoes, in a good oven. Eat it with either boiled onions, currant or jelly sauce.

BOILED MUTTON.—A leg of mutton requires two hours' boiling; a leg of lamb, one hour. All fresh meat must be put on in hot water; if it has been salted, lay it first in cold water, and gradually heat it. Mint sauce or caper sauce should accompany it. Make the caper sauce in this way: Chop the capers very small, add some of the gravy of the mutton, thicken it with a tablespoonful of flour, two beaten eggs, then boil all together, and serve the same in a sauce-bowl. Mutton with turnips can be cooked in this way.

HOW TO BROIL A STEAK.—Have a very clear fire; if it should be smoky, throw some salt on the top and it will clear it. Let the grid iron be placed on the fire and made very hot; wipe it well; put the meat on it, not too close to the fire, and turn it frequently, be careful not to prick the meat, but the fat part. If you use a double grid iron, you can turn it better; then put it on a dish; strew some salt and pepper over it. Serve it hot. Have the plates and dishes made warm.

A NICE DISH OF LAMB.—Take the best end of a neck of lamb, cut it into chops, and chop each bone so short as to make the chops almost round. Egg and strew with crumbs, herbs, and seasoning. Fry them a nice brown. Mash some potatoes, and put them in the middle of the dish, raised high; then place the edge of one chop on another, with the small bone upward, around the potatoes.

CALF'S PLUCK AND MARGEN.—Well cleanse some nice tripe, and cut it up small, place it in a saucepan with one pound of meat, cut up small, and stew for four or five hours; when it is tender, put it away in a cool place until the next day; then put it in a saucepan with some gravy; adding chopped parsley, thyme, marjoram, salt, cayenne pepper, and suet dumplings, made rather small; prepare in the following manner the milt, after it has been porged, (that is, take out the veins,) and (כשר) coshered, cleansed from the blood: Scrape all the insides out very fine, chop a quarter of a pound of suet, some bread crumbs, parsley, thyme, marjoram, and a (reished) fried onion, cut small; season with salt, cayenne, ginger, nutmeg, and mix the ingredients all together with an egg, and return it all back to the skin of the milt and sew it up; put it with the tripe to stew for three hours. Before dishing thicken the gravy with a little flour.

PUREE OF PEAS.—Take a quart of marrow fat peas and boil them with some mint, a few young onions, some chopped parsley; then strain off the water, and pound the whole well in a mortar; take it up and put it in a stewpan, adding a little sugar, some butter or meat, gravy thickened with a tablespoonful of flour, a little pepper and salt; warm it over a gentle fire.

PUREE OF CHESTNUTS.—Pare and clean about one hundred chestnuts, and set them in a stewpan on a gentle fire, with some good prepared gravy; keep the lid on, and let them stew on one corner of the stove; when they are done beat them well in a mortar; take them up in a pan, add a little nutmeg and sugar; if they are not intended to be eaten with meat, the gravy must be left out and cream used instead; then return it to the stewpan, and make it hot; add a lump of butter.

PUREE OF MUSHROOMS.—Clean a quart of white button mushrooms, chop them fine, add a teaspoonful of lemon juice to keep them white; then put them in a stewpan with a lump of butter, and stir with a silver spoon for ten minutes; add some white sauce to it and let it stew gently, then add half a pint of good cream, stir it for ten minutes longer, strain and return it to the stewpan, and make it hot to dish up.

TO STEW A BRISKET WITH STRING BEANS.—Take a piece, according to the size of the family. Put a pint and a half of water in a saucepan, with about six large onions, and let them come to a boil; then skim it well, and place the beans cut small in the saucepan, with some ginger, salt, and pepper, and stew them until tender. Half an hour before dishing, add a half pint of vinegar, a tablespoonful of coarse sugar, and a tablespoonful of flour, thickened, and let it boil for ten minutes. Dish up, and send it to the table hot.

HASH OF COLD MEAT.—Take some cold meat that has been either boiled or roasted, and cut it very fine, not chopped. Put it to some made gravy, with ginger, pepper, mace, salt, a little nutmeg, a little grated lemon-peel, and a few cold potatoes, with a little lemon juice, and sweet herbs. Let them stew gently, with two onions. Dish up with sippets of toasted bread. It can be fried into balls, with the addition of an egg, beaten up, and some grated bread crumbs, and made into fritters. To be eaten with a little lemon juice.

VEAL OLIVES.—Cut long thin collops; beat them; lay them on thin slices of smoked beef, and over these a layer of forcemeat, highly seasoned, with some shred shallot and cayenne. Roll them tight, about the size of two fingers, cut them about two inches long; fasten them round with a small skewer; rub egg over them, and fry them of a light brown. Serve with brown gravy, in which boil some mushrooms, pickled or fresh. Garnish with balls fried.

TO BOIL CALF'S HEAD.—Clean it very nicely, and soak it in water, that it may look very white. Boil the head extremely tender; then strew it over with some bread crumbs and chopped parsley, and brown them; or if preferred, leave one side plain. Serve with smoked meat. The brains must be boiled, and then mixed with some chopped fat, marjoram, parsley, salt, pepper, bread crumbs, and eggs.

TO COOK LIVER.—Lay it in water half an hour; then take it out of the water and sprinkle salt over it, and broil it over a clear fire; then rinse it in cold water to cleanse it from the blood. Cut it up in thin slices, and fry with plenty of fat and onions; season with pepper and salt. To be eaten hot.

The liver of a goose may be prepared in this way, after the above process of cleansing from the blood: chop the liver very fine, add an onion, pepper, and salt, and fry in goose fat. Very relishing on a piece of bread.

TO COOK THE LIGHTS AND HEART OF A CALF.—Cut the lights very small, with a pound of beef, and set it on the fire in a saucepan, with a pint of water, some pepper, salt, ginger, an onion, and parsley. Let them stew gently; when done, add a tablespoonful of flour, and a tablespoonful of vinegar, to thicken. To be eaten with mashed potatoes. The heart must be made (כשר) cosher, then well washed. Season it with some sage and onions, and make a stuffing in the following manner: chop some sage, well dried, an onion, bread crumbs, and suet, some salt and pepper, rub some flour and salt outside the heart, and roast with plenty of fat. When it is done, dip it in a pan of boiling water, or pour boiling water over it, to make the gravy. Be careful to have the dish and plates made very hot, as the fat is apt to stick to the roof of the mouth, but dipping it in water will prevent that.

VEAL SAUSAGE MEAT.—Take a nice, fat piece of veal, clear of skin and sinews, and chop it fine, with some beef suet, one half pound of tender steak, and some bread crumbs, pepper and salt.

LAMB CUTLETS, WITH SPINACH.—Fry the cutlets a nice brown, with bread crumbs and egg. Stew some spinach; then strain it, and chop it fine with some onions; add a tablespoonful of flour, a little pepper and salt, with some good gravy; arrange the spinach around the cutlets.

HARICOT STEW, WITH BEANS.—Take a nice piece of beef and a quart of dried beans; stew with some cayenne pepper and salt in a quart of water, until tender, and thicken with a tablespoonful of flour.

VEAL OR CHICKEN CURRY.—Cut up a good, fat chicken in small pieces, and some veal and beef; let them stew gently in two quarts of water, and six ounces of rice; season with pepper, salt, and one good tablespoonful of curry. Three or four onions will improve the flavor; for those who like them. Dish up and send to the table hot. Line the dish with the rice, and set the chicken, etc., in the middle. Any cold meat or chicken would be good cooked in this way.

COLD MEAT HASH.—Any cold, salt meat or mutton that is left can be cooked in the following manner: the meat to be cut very small, and the potatoes previously cooked; put them all in a saucepan, with a pint of cold water; season with pepper, salt, ginger, a little grated nutmeg, and stew gentle for a couple of hours. A tablespoonful of vinegar, thickened with a little flour, will add to the flavor.

ROAST VEAL WITH OLIVE OIL AND LEMONS.—Take a good sized fillet of veal; prepare as other roast beef or veal; baste it before a good open fire, with a pint of sweet oil and the juice of two lemons. Dish up very hot. Pour some boiling water in the gravy, and baste for half an hour, before dishing.

MEAT STEWED WITH RAISINS AND APPLES.—Take a good piece of fat meat, and put it in a saucepan, with some seasoning; add one pound of raisins, and a quart of good sized apples. Stew all together, in a quart and a pint of water, till tender; thicken with a tablespoonful of flour. Be careful that it does not burn.

TONGUE WITH SAUER KRAUT.—Soak a smoked tongue in water for six hours before cooking it; parboil it for half an hour in cold water, then take off the root, put a skewer in it to keep it in shape, then put it in the stewpan, with about a pound and a half of sauer kraut, well washed, with two carrots, two onions, ten cloves, and a bunch of parsley, cover it with some stock; let it stew gently for three or four hours; when the tongue is done take it out and trim it, then remove the carrots and parsley, and dish up. Garnish with carrots arranged around the dish.

GRAVY.—When there is any fear of meat gravy being spoiled before it is used, season well, this will preserve it two days longer; yet it is best always when freshly made.

SWEET BREADS.—Blanch them, and let them stand a little while in cold water. Then put them in a stewpan, with a ladleful of water, some pepper, salt, onions, and mace. Stew them half an hour. Have ready two or three eggs, well beaten, with a little chopped parsley, and a few grates of nutmeg. Put in some small boiled asparagus to the other ingredients.

MINT SAUCE.—*For roast lamb may be made in the following manner:* Half a pint of vinegar, a tablespoonful of sugar, with some mint, chopped fine.

WOSHT, OR SAUSAGE AND RICE.—Wash and pick half a pound of rice, and put it on with cold water. Do not stir the rice while boiling; let it cook gently; add a tablespoonful of salt and ginger. When it is nearly cooked put in the sausage, and let it boil for half an hour. Fried in slices and dished with poached eggs on top, is very good. A little dried saffron may be added to color it.

GERMAN SWEET SAUCE.—Put six ounces of dried cherries in two glasses of red wine, and stew them with ground cinnamon, cloves and lemon peel, for half an hour on a gentle fire, then strain then through a sieve, and put it back in a stewpan, with some brown gravy, and a quarter of a pound of prunes. This sauce is very fine for roast mutton.

CHERRY SAUCE.—Place a pot of black currant jelly in a stewpan, with six ounces of dried cherries, a little bit of stick cinnamon, six cloves, and half a pint of red wine; let it all stew gently on a slow fire for fifteen minutes; take out the spices, and dish it up for leg of mutton.

GERMIES.—Boil some cabbage very tender; after it is done strain and chop it up, season it with fried onions, pepper, salt and ginger, and a little nutmeg, thicken with a tablespoonful of flour, fry in fat. Send to table hot.

A LITTLE ENTREE DISH.—Boil some eggs hard; soak a dutch herring for one hour, then skin and cut it up in small slices and put it on a dish; then arrange the egg, cut in slices, around the herring.

GOOD SAUCE FOR COLD ROAST BEEF.—Grate some horseradish, mix with it a little made mustard, some pounded sugar, and four large spoonfuls of vinegar.

BEEF TEA.—*For a very weak person recovering from fever:* Take two pounds of good juicy beef, and chop it very fine; have ready some gravy made of calf's feet, and place the chopped meat in a jar along with the gravy, place it in a saucepan of water, and put it on a slow fire; let the water boil under the jar for two hours, then strain off the juice; season with some ginger and salt, not too highly.

POTATO STEW.—Take some stock and boil it with about three pounds of potatoes, cut into small pieces, not sliced, and when cooked, add two tablespoonfuls of vinegar, and a little flour to thicken; season it well, and dish up hot.

HORSERADISH STEW.—Stew three pounds of meat in a pint of water; grate one large horseradish, add it to the gravy and some fine bread crumbs, a little pepper, ginger and salt, with half a cupful of the best vinegar. It is very highly recommended by all who have tasted it.

GOOD STEW WITHOUT WATER.—Take a nice, juicy piece of meat, three or four pounds of bola, put it into a saucepan with some onions, reished or fried, and plenty of good fat, pepper ginger and salt; cover it down close, and let it cook on a gentle fire for four or five hours.

MUTTON STEWED WITH TURNIPS.—Take a piece of nice fat meat, about four pounds, stew in a pint of water until tender; when it has come to a boil, have some young turnips sliced, and put them in with the meat to stew gently; when nearly done take some pepper, salt, a teaspoonful of sugar, and a cupful of vinegar thickened with flour, add it to the stew, and let it cook for ten minutes.

SPICED BEEF.—Take a piece of flank, about eight pounds, without any bones, and (כשר) cosher it as in directions; after it is coshered, rub it well with salt and let it lay in pickle for three or four days; then take half an ounce of whole cloves, half an ounce of black pepper, half an ounce of Jamaica ginger, half a teaspoonful of cayenne pepper, some chopped parsley, thyme and marjoram, spread it over the beef; then roll it up and tie tightly; set it in a saucepan of cold water, and let it boil for four hours till tender, then press it well; it is best eaten cold.

HOW TO ROLL A BREAST OF VEAL.—Bone a piece of the breast weighing about six pounds, and prepare some grated bread crumbs with chopped parsley, fried onions, a little ginger, salt, chopped suet, marjoram and thyme, mix all together with two well beaten eggs; then roll out the veal, and place the above preparation inside; roll it up tightly, and tie it with a string in an oval shape; it can be either roasted or stewed in this way; if roasted use plenty of melted fat to baste it.

POTTED BEEF.—Take about seven or eight pounds of beef, and half a pound of fat, add pepper, salt, ginger and mace; put it into a stone jar with half a pint of cold water; stand the jar in a deep stewpan of boiling water to boil slowly for eight hours, taking care that the water does not reach to the top of the jar; when it is done take it out and mince it fine; when it is smooth and like a paste, mix in some of the gravy and some fat; press it into the pots, and pour on top clarified or melted fat, tie it down tightly, and keep it in a cool place.

CUCUMBER STEW.—Take a piece of steak, about two or three pounds, and fry it a nice brown, with some onions. Have ready a stewpan, with a pint of water, seasoned with pepper and salt. Then take a good sized cucumber, pare it, cut it into long strips, and fry it a nice brown, put into the stew when done; then add some soy, a tablespoonful of vinegar, and mushroom ketchup, thickened with browned flour; or scoop out all the seeds of a large cucumber, and fill it in with forcemeat. Serve with forcemeat balls around the dish.

TOMATO STEW.—Cut up some steak, with ten or twelve large tomatoes and some onions; smother the tomatoes with the meat; add some salt and pepper; put no water in this stew, but use a little melted fat, and thicken with a tablespoonful of flour.

EIN GEFULLTER MAGEN.—Grate a small stale loaf, chop up some parsley, and (reish) fry two onions in a quarter of a pound of fat, mix them together and place inside the magen or stomach; sew it up securely; then put it in a stewpan with a quart of water, let it cook very slowly for three or four hours; the addition of a piece of beef would improve the flavor; season with salt, pepper, ginger mace, a little grated nutmeg, two or three onions, a small piece of garlic. Previous to dishing up for table, take it out of the saucepan and fry it a light brown.

HOW TO MAKE SAUER KROUT.—Cut the cabbage fine, pack it tight in a clean barrel, with salt between each layer of cabbage, pound it down very tight, then lay a weight on the top, and place the cover on tight, put it in a warm cellar for three weeks, then take off the skum which will rise on the top, and lay a clean cloth on; the juice should always cover the krout. It will keep for years.

TOAD IN A HOLE.—Take either a chicken or shoulder of mutton, and fill it with a veal stuffing; then make a batter with a quart of water and six eggs, and sufficient flour to make it thick; season with a tablespoonful of salt and a tablespoonful of ginger; pour it into a well greased pan, and place the mutton or chicken in the centre, and bake in an oven; put plenty of fat on top of the chicken; serve it up on the same dish.

POTTED OX TONGUE.—Remove the skin from a fresh tongue that has been boiled quite tender; pound it in a mortar as fine as possible, with a quarter of a pound of chopped suet, and season with salt, ginger, allspice, nutmeg, cayenne pepper and mace; when well pounded and the spice well mixed with the meat, press it into small pots, and pour melted fat over the top; a little roasted veal added to the tongue is a great improvement.

CALF'S BRAIN AND PIGEON, Stewed with Green Peas.—Cut about four calves' brains in slices, and fry them in a batter of egg and flour a light brown; put them in a stewpan with a pint and a half of water; split four pigeons in half and quarter them; season with pepper, ginger, mace, nutmeg, chopped parsley and salt; three-quarters of an hour before dishing up, add a pint of marrow-fat green peas and one quart of button mushrooms; stew all gently for two hours.

POULTRY.

To choose Poultry.

A Turkey.—If young it has a smooth, black leg, with a short spur, and the eyes are full and bright; if fresh, the feet are supple and moist; if stale, the eyes will be sunk and the feet dry.

Chickens.—If a rooster is young, his spurs will be short; but take care to see they have not been pared or cut—a trick often practised. If fresh, the vent will be close and dark. Pullets are best just before laying eggs; they are old if full of eggs. If hens are old, their legs will be rough; if young, they will be smooth. A good capon has a thick and large belly. There is a particular fat at his breast, and the comb is very pale. Black legged fowls are best if for roasting.

Geese.—The bill and feet of a young goose will be yellow, and there will be few hairs upon them; if old, they will be red; if fresh, the feet will be pliable; if stale, dry and stiff. Geese are called green until three or four months old.

Ducks.—Choose by the same rules of having supple feet, and by being hard and thick on the breast and belly.

Directions for Dressing Poultry.

All poultry should be very carefully picked, every plug removed, and the hair singed. You must be careful, in drawing the poultry, not to break the gall-bag, for no washing will take off the bitterness where it has once touched. Be sure to baste well and often, as that will improve the flavor. Do not cook them too much, just enough to look a nice brown, as they will lose their flavor if too much done. A large chicken will take an hour in a quick oven; a goose an hour and a half to two hours gentle cooking.

TO BOIL A TURKEY.—Make a stuffing of bread crumbs, salt, pepper, ginger, nutmeg, a little mace, some chopped suet, parsley, and an egg. Mix all together, and put it in the crop, fasten up the skin; boil the turkey in a floured cloth, to make it white. Have ready some of the liver, chopped up fine, and the juice of two lemons, strained, with two eggs, beaten. Take some of the gravy from the turkey soup and add it to the lemon juice. Do not boil the egg with the gravy, thicken the gravy with a tablespoonful of flour; when done add the gravy to the uncooked egg and stir it all together; dish up in a gravy boat.

TO ROAST TURKEY.—The sinews of the leg should be drawn, whichever way it is dressed. Put a filling of sausage meat in the breast, or stuff, as for roast. A piece of white paper should be put on the bone to prevent scorching while the other parts roast. Baste it well, and dredge with flour while basting. Serve it up with nice gravy. Garnish with veal sausage.

TO BOIL FOWLS.—For boiling do not choose those that are black legged. Flour them and put them into boiling water for an hour and a half. Serve with chopped parsley, the same as turkey, or celery sauce. Smoked beef is generally eaten with it, or smoked tongue.

TO BOIL A FOWL WITH RICE.—Stew it in some good beef broth, well skimmed, seasoned with onion, mace, pepper, ginger, and salt. About half an hour before it is cooked, put in a quarter of a pound of rice, well washed and picked; simmer till tender; then strain the rice from the broth, and put the rice on a sieve before the fire. Keep the fowl hot; lay it in the dish, and the rice around it, with the gravy; the broth will be nice to drink, with some griebs made from an egg and flour, rubbed fine; a little saffron may be added to color. The less gravy the fowl is cooked in the better.

ROAST DUCKS.—Chop up some sage and onions; put the onions in an oven; let them cook to take the strength out of them, and chop them very fine, with some grated bread crumbs, cayenne pepper, salt, and a little chopped suet; put this in the breast of the duck, rub some flour, pepper, and salt over it, and set it in the pan to bake, with plenty of fat to baste with. When done, pour off the fat, and add half a pint of hot water and flour to the pan; let it boil up for a minute; then dish up. Be sure to have all the plates and dishes made warm, in the screen, half an hour before dinner.

Geese can be dressed the same way, and eaten with apple sauce; gooseberry sauce for a green goose.

GERMAN CHICKEN STEW.—Cut up a good sized chicken in small pieces, and put them in a saucepan, with a quart of water. Let it stew till tender; season with pepper, ginger, salt, chopped parsley, sweet herbs, and a little garlic; thicken with a tablespoonful of flour. Dish up, and garnish with lemon, parsley, and boiled carrots.

TO ROAST A CHICKEN.—Cosher (כשר) and prepare a chicken, and put it into the pan, floured with a little ginger and salt, and put some melted fat on the top of the chicken; baste frequently while roasting. Take a good portion of the fat off, and add a little water, thickened with flour; return the chicken to the oven, and baste well for ten minutes before dishing. Make the seasoning as follows: take half a pound of bread crumbs, parsley, thyme, and marjoram, half a teaspoonful of cayenne pepper, ginger, and salt, some melted fat, and one egg. Mix all together, and fill the chicken with it. Make your stuffing as large as will do for a family. Some persons like reished onions in the seasoning, they will improve the flavor.

GIBLET PIE.—Take two pounds of beef, and cut it small. Set it on in a stewpan with some onions, parsley, marjoram, thyme, pepper, mace, salt, ginger, and a little nutmeg, and let it all stew till tender. Then make a light crust, with three-quarters of a pound of flour, half a pound of fat, melted, and a little salt, in the following manner: take a portion of the fat and rub it in the flour very fine, and a half pint of water, and mix, not too stiff nor too soft, and roll out thin; add the remainder of the fat by laying it on the dough, in layers, and dust it well with flour, roll out several times; then line the dish with some of the paste, rolled very thin, place the meat and giblets inside with the gravy, leaving out a portion to add when the pie is baked a nice brown color. Put on the top three or four hard boiled eggs, cut in slices, and some potatoes, thinly sliced. When the pie is nearly done, take the yolk of an egg, well beaten, and with a feather spread the egg over the top, to glaze it. Keep out some of the gravy to add to the pie when baked, pour it in by lifting the crust a little.

GIBLET STEW.—Take a piece of beef of three pounds, and cut it small. Wash the giblets of some ducks, geese, or turkey, such as gizzard, liver, wings, neck, etc., and cut them quite small; fry some onions in suet; then fry the meat and giblets, and put all in a saucepan with a pint of water; add ginger, pepper, salt, a little cayenne pepper, mace, and parsley. Stew until tender. Mix a tablespoonful of browned flour with a little mushroom ketchup, and some forcemeat balls. Dish up hot, with some hard boiled eggs round the dish.

GIBLET PUDDING.—Make your pastry as follows: three quarters of a pound of suet chopped very fine, rub this smoothly into one pound of flour, add a teaspoonful of salt, one of ginger, and mixed with sufficient water to make a paste, strew with flour and pound well with the rolling-pin, then roll out very thin, repeating this three times, line the pudding bowl with this pastry, which should be about one-quarter of an inch in thickness; put in the following giblets: two pounds of meat, cut very small, the necks, wings, gizzards, livers, and head, that has been split open and the skin taken off the brain, and the feet skinned and the claws chopped off; all to be cut up small. Season with marjoram, thyme, parsley, onions, pepper, salt, mace, ginger, and a few potatoes out in very thin slices, with hard boiled eggs. Then cover the top of the basin with the above paste, and tie tightly in a cloth, put in boiling water and boil for three hours.

COOGLE, OR PUDDING, AND PEAS AND BEANS.—Take a shin bone and a piece of bola, about three pounds; get a pint of Spanish beans, others will serve the same, and a pint of Spanish peas; put them in a brown pan, one that will fit the oven, and put the beef, peas, and beans in it, and cover it over with water; add pepper, ginger, salt, and a little cayenne pepper. Make the coogle in the following manner: a quarter of a pound of currants, a quarter of a pound of raisins, a quarter of a pound of sugar, the same quantity of bread crumbs and suet, chopped fine, four eggs, a quarter of a pound of flour, some spices and a small piece of citron. Mix well together; put the coogle (or pudding) in a basin, place it in the pan with the peas and beans, and cover the pudding basin with a plate. Let it cook a day and night, and dish up the soup without the meat. Some persons like the meat, others do not. Turn out the pudding and eat with a sauce. Be sure while cooking this dish, to see there is sufficient water on it; if plenty is put on at first, it will not require much when cooking.

FOWLS, BROILED.—Half roast the fowl whole, and then split it and finish on the gridiron, which will make it less dry than if it was wholly broiled. When done, season it with some pepper and salt.

TO FRICASSEE CHICKEN.—Cut the chicken up, and lay the pieces in a saucepan, with enough water to cover them; season it well; after it has boiled a few minutes, skim the surface, and add pepper. When the chicken is boiled tender, take the pieces out, and pour off the water, if there is too much for gravy. When the chickens are fat, they require no suet. Lay the chicken back in the saucepan, and thicken with flour, and see it is seasoned sufficient.

POACHED EGGS.—Set a stewpan on the fire with water. When boiling, slip an egg, previously broken, into a cup in the water. When the white looks done enough, slide an egg-slice under the egg, and lay it on toast or spinach. Serve hot; trim the ragged part off the whites, and make them look round.

BUTTERED EGGS.—Beat four or five eggs, yolks and whites together. Put a quarter of a pound of butter in a basin, and then put that in boiling water; stir it till melted; then pour the butter and the eggs into a saucepan. Keep a basin in one hand, and hold the saucepan in the other hand, over a slow part of the fire, shaking it one way. As it begins to warm, pour it into a basin and back; then hold it again over the fire, stirring it constantly in the saucepan, and pouring it in the basin to mix the egg and butter more perfectly, until they shall be hot, without boiling. Serve hot, on toasted bread, or in a basin. To be eaten with salt fish or herring.

CHICKEN SALAD.—Cut up some cold fowl, and make a sauce as for herbs, or lettuce; chopped parsley, onions, celery, and hardboiled eggs. Cover over with the sauce, as directed for herb sauce. The onions may be left out, if not liked.

CUCUMBER SALAD.—Pare and cut the cucumbers in very thin slices, and some onions. Let them stand for one hour before they are wanted, and then pour off the water quite dry; then mix together, two tablespoonfuls of vinegar, a teaspoonful of salad oil, pepper and salt, and throw over them.

Any string beans or cold cabbage can be made into very nice salads.

SALADS.—The herbs should be nice and fresh. They will improve in flavor by laying in spring water an hour or two. It is very important that they should be carefully washed, picked, and dried, before using. Prepare them in this way: boil two eggs for twelve minutes, and then put them in cold water for a few minutes, so that the yolks may become quite cold and hard; rub the yolks quite fine with a wooden spoon. If for supper, mix them with a tablespoonful of cream, and then add one or two tablespoonfuls of the best flask oil; add, by degrees, a tablespoonful of salt, and the same quantity of mustard; mix till smooth. When well mixed with the other ingredients, add about three tablespoonfuls of vinegar; then pour this sauce in a salad bowl, but do not stir up the salad until wanted to be eaten. Garnish with slices of bread, boiled eggs, slices of beet root, and chopped white of eggs; then cut in quarters, and put on top.

SALAD OF POTATOES.—Take some cold potatoes, and slice them very fine; add some chopped parsley and onions. Prepare the same sauce as for herb salad.

SWEET OMELET, No. 1.—Take four eggs, well beaten, two tablespoonfuls of milk, and a pinch of salt. Have ready a small piece of butter in a frying pan, and fry it a nice brown; hold it over a salamander to brown the top. Fold it up, and send it quite hot to table.

SWEET OMELET, No. 2.—(Mix as No. 1.) Add to it a little chopped parsley and green onions, a little pepper salt, and a little smoked beef, or sausage, fried in fat instead of butter. If for dinner, water may be substituted for milk. Four eggs will make a good sized omelet. Extravagant cooks will use eight or ten. Plenty of parsley may be used in this omelet.

OMELET.—Beat up four eggs with two tablespoonfuls of sweet milk and a little salt and pepper; beat whites and yolks separately; put a small piece of butter into the frying pan, let it get very hot, pour in the mixture, move the pan to and fro; then hold the pan still a minute or two to give the omelet a nice color, then turn it into a dish for table.

EGGS AND CHEESE.—Spread the bottom of a dish with two ounces of fresh butter, cover this with rather thin slices of fresh Parmesan cheese, break eight eggs upon the cheese without disturbing the yolks; season with grated nutmeg, cayenne pepper and salt; pour two tablespoonfuls of cream on the top; strew the top with about two ounces of the cheese, grated, and set the eggs in the oven to bake for a quarter of an hour; press the salamander over the top, and serve it with thin toast separately on a plate.

WELSH RABBIT OR WELSH RARE BIT.—Toast a slice of bread on both sides and butter it; toast a slice of English cheese on one side, lay it next to the bread, and toast the other with a salamander; rub mustard over and serve very hot.

A NICE SUPPER DISH.—Equal quantities of Parmesan cheese and English cheese, and double the weight of these in beaten yolks of eggs and melted butter; beat all together well. Add pepper and salt; then put in the whites of the eggs, which have been beaten to a thick snow, separately; stir them lightly.

ANCHOVY TOAST.—Bone and skin six or eight anchovies, pound them with an ounce of butter until the color is equal, and then spread it on fresh made thin toast or rusk.

HOW TO FATTEN POULTRY in four or five days.—Boil some rice with skimmed milk, only as much as will serve one day; let it boil, with a teaspoonful of sugar, until the rice is swelled out. Feed them three times a day, in common pans, giving them as much as will quite fill them at one time. Before putting fresh food into the pans wash them clean, so that no sour food may be given to the poultry, as it will prevent them getting fat. Give them clean water, or the milk off the rice to drink, but the less water the better; by this method the flesh will have a clear whiteness, which no other food gives it. The pen should always be kept clean, and no food given them for sixteen hours before killing.

MACARONI.—Boil the macaroni in milk well flavored with salt; when it is tender put it in a dish without the liquor, and add to it some pieces of butter and grated cheese, and over the top put a little more cheese and butter; set the dish in a Dutch oven for a quarter of an hour, but do not let the top become hard.

BREAD.

TO MAKE YEAST.—Thicken two quarts of water with about three spoonfuls of fine flour, boil half an hour, sweeten with half a pound of brown sugar; when nearly cold put four spoonfuls of fresh yeast in a pitcher, shake it well together, and let it stand near the fire, without a cover one day, to ferment. There will be a thin liquor on the top, which must be poured off; shake the remainder and cork it for use; always take four spoonfuls of the old to ferment the next quantity. A four pound loaf will require a gill of yeast.

SPONGE FOR BREAD.—(*It is best to set it over night.*) Pour three quarts of milk-warm water into a pan large enough to make your bread, throw in one tablespoonful of salt and stir in some good yeast, (in warm weather do not use so much yeast,) about a cupful; thicken with flour until it is of a soft batter, put it in a warm place; if the weather is cool cover it with a clean cloth; in the morning, if the sponge is sour dissolve a large teaspoonful of saleratus in a little cold water and stir it in, if it still seems sour add more, work in flour, and knead the dough thoroughly, making it into small loaves; the pans must be well greased and warmed when used; place the loaves in a warm place and keep covered with a warm white cloth; if properly seen to, the bread will be nice and light in an hour and ready to bake in a good hot oven. Do not let the top of the bread scorch or brown too soon, as it will prevent its rising up light.

EXCELLENT CORN BREAD.—Three quarts of sour milk, seven eggs, one cup of melted butter, one teaspoonful of saleratus, mix with corn meal to the consistency of a thick batter, and bake in a brisk oven.

WHEAT BREAD.—Three quarts of water, luke-warm, a spoonful of salt, half a pint of light yeast; stir in enough flour to make a thick batter, then let it stand to rise. After it is light enough add more flour to it, and knead it well into loaves; then put it in pans greased with olive oil. When it rises sufficiently a second time, bake about three-quarters of an hour in a thoroughly heated oven.

POTATO BREAD.—Take two pounds of fine flour and rub it into one pound of warm mashed potatoes; then mix some warm milk and water with a little yeast and salt, and put it in the flour; let it rise for two hours in a warm place in winter; bake it in tins. It makes nice rolls for breakfast. By adding some sugar, eggs and currants, you can make nice buns.

SCOTCH SHORT BREAD.—One pound of flour, one pound of white sugar, one pound of butter, eight eggs, half a pound of candied lemon peel, orange and citron, the same proportions, two tablespoonfuls of cognac brandy, and three ounces of white comfits; beat the butter with a wooden spoon to a cream; then add the flour, sugar, eggs, a little salt, throwing in a little at a time; when it is all well mixed put in the lemon-peel, cut in shreds, the brandy and two rinds of lemon, grated. This paste must be put into tins of an oblong shape, about two inches deep, greased with good butter. Strew the comfits on the top, with some white sifted sugar. Bake on sheets of iron a light brown.

TWIST BREAD.—Let the bread be made as directed for wheat bread; strew a little flour over the paste board; then take three good sized pieces of dough, and roll each piece under your hands, twelve inches long, making it smaller in circumference at the ends than in the middle; having rolled the pieces in this way, take a baking dish and lay one part on it, join one end of each of the other two to it, and braid them together the length of the rolls, then join the ends by pressing them together; dip a brush in milk, and pass it over the top of the loaf; after ten minutes or so set it in a quick oven, and bake for nearly an hour.

FRENCH BREAD.—With a quarter of a peck of fine flour mix the yolks of three eggs and the whites of two, well beaten, a little salt, half a pint of good yeast, that is not bitter, and as much milk, warmed, as will work into a thin, light dough; stir it around, but do not knead it. Prepare three quart wooden dishes; divide the dough in three parts, and let it rise; bake in a quick oven. Rasp when done.

COMMON BREAD CAKE.—Take two pounds of bread dough, when making white bread, and knead it well with two ounces of butter, two ounces of brown sugar, and half a pound of currants; warm the butter and put it in a cupful of milk, add a couple of eggs. Bake it in a pan.

FRENCH ROLLS.—Rub an ounce of butter into a pound of flour, mix one egg, beaten, a little yeast, not bitter, and as much milk as will make dough of a middling stiffness; beat it well, but do not knead; let it rise; and bake in tin pans.

POTATO ROLLS.—Boil three pounds of potatoes, bruise and work them with two ounces of butter and as much milk as will make them pass through a colander ; take half or three-quarters of a pint of yeast and half a pint of warm water, mix with the potatoes; then pour the whole upon five pounds of flour, and add some salt. Knead it well; if not of a proper consistence, add a little more milk and warm water; let it stand before the fire an hour to rise; work it well and make it into rolls. Bake about half an hour in an oven not quite so hot as for bread. They eat well toasted and buttered.

TEA ROLLS.—Two teaspoonfuls of saleratus, one teaspoonful of soda, half a pint of sour milk, a small piece of butter, a pound of flour, a teaspoonful of salt; mix all well together, and cut in small cakes; bake in a quick oven.

HARD BISCUIT.—Warm two ounces of butter in as much skimmed milk as will work up a pound of flour into a very stiff paste; beat it with a rolling pin, and knead it very smooth; roll it thin, and cut it into round biscuits; prick holes in the biscuit with a fork; bake about six minutes.

HOT BISCUITS.—Rub into a pound of flour six ounces of butter and three large spoonfuls of yeast, add a sufficient quantity of milk to make a nice dough; knead it into biscuits, and prick them with a fork; bake in a moderate oven.

CREAM OF TARTAR BISCUITS.—One quart of flour, two teaspoonfuls of cream of tartar, one of saleratus, two and a half cups of milk, and a small piece of butter; bake in small pans for twenty minutes.

BISCUIT OF FRUIT.—To the pulp of any scalded fruit add an equal weight of sifted sugar, beat it well, then put it into little white paper forms and dry in a cool oven; turn them the next day, and in two or three days box them.

PLAIN AND VERY CRISP CRACKERS.—Mix a pound of flour, the yolk of an egg, and some milk, into a stiff paste; beat it well and knead till quite smooth, then roll very thin and cut into crackers. Bake them in a slow oven till quite dry and crisp.

APPLE FRITTERS.—Peel and core six large apples, cut them in thin slices, soak them in wine and sugar for two hours, then make a batter of four eggs, a teaspoonful of rose water, or essence of lemon, a tablespoonful of wine, and a cup of milk, add three ounces of flour, mixed in by degrees. Heat some butter in a pan; dip each slice of apple in the batter and fry a nice brown; sift powdered sugar and a little nutmeg over them.

SALERATUS FRITTERS.—A teaspoonful of saleratus, half a pound of flour, a pint of milk, a little salt, two eggs, well beaten; mix all together, and fry with plenty of butter or sweet oil to a light brown color. To be eaten hot with sauce or sifted sugar.

HOMINY FRITTERS.—Have some hominy previously boiled, and when cold make this into fritters; put cinnamon and nutmeg upon them, and fry either in butter or fat; serve with wine sauce, jelly, or preserved fruit.

BREAD FRITTERS.—Soak two or three slices of bread in milk, then mix with some apples, previously stewed, sugar, cinnamon, nutmeg, the rind of a lemon, grated, and two eggs, well beaten; make them into fritters, and fry them in butter; then strew white sugar on top. To be served hot.

BUCKWHEAT CAKES.—One quart of buckwheat flour, one-half cup of yeast, one tablespoonful of salt, nearly a quart and a half of warm water; beat well with a large spoon; let the batter rise over night; in the morning add a teaspoonful of saleratus, and fry on a griddle greased with a piece of rag.

WAFFLES can be made with a thin batter of eggs, milk and flour, or boiled hominy; baked on the waffle-irons over the fire a nice brown color.

MUFFINS.—Mix two pounds of flour with two eggs, two ounces of butter, melted, in a pint of milk, and four or five spoonfuls of yeast; beat it thoroughly, and set it to rise three hours; bake in rings, in a hot oven. When done on one side turn them.

Muffins, rolls, or bread, if stale, may be made soft and the freshness renewed by dipping in cold water and heating over in the oven, or Dutch oven, till the outside is crisp.

CAKES.

Observations on making Pastry or Cakes.

The best way to make light cakes is always to take the fruit, flour, and spices, and mix well together first; then take the butter and sugar and beat to a cream; beat the eggs, yolks and whites, separately; add them to the butter and sugar; then mix the other ingredients in slowly, until properly concentrated; beat for half an hour, and bake in a hot oven. Be careful to observe these rules, and you will succeed in making good cakes. The heat of the oven is important; it must always be quick, or the batter will not rise. To prevent it from burning, place a piece of white paper on the top. Use a clean knife or straw when trying if the cake is properly cooked. Cakes must be well soaked in a gentle oven.

AN ICE CAKE.—For a large one, mix eight ounces of finely sifted flour with four spoonfuls of rose water, the whites of eggs, whisked to a snow; when the cake is almost cold, dip a feather in the icing, and pass it over the cake; set it in the oven to harden, but do not let it stay too long or it will become discolored. Put the cake in a dry place.

TO ICE A VERY LARGE CAKE.—Beat the whites of twenty eggs, by degrees, in a pound of double refined sugar; mix these well in a deep earthenware pan; add orange flower water, and a piece of lemon peel, enough flower water to flavor and no more; whisk it for three hours, till the mixture is thick and white; then, with a thin, broad bit of board, spread it over the top and sides, and set it in a cool oven; an hour will harden it.

A RICH SODA CAKE.—Mix together one pound of flour, one pound of chopped raisins, one pound of currants, or half a pound will do, a quarter of a pound of citron, a quarter of a pound of blanched almonds, one pound of butter, one pound of brown sugar, the rind of one lemon, one pint of milk, five eggs, one teaspoonful of soda mixed in the flour, and any flavoring spices that are preferred.

A PLAIN SODA CAKE, No. 1.—Follow the same directions as above, with the omission of the fruit.

A PLAIN SODA CAKE, No. 2.—Beat together one egg, half a pound of butter, one cup of sweet milk, dissolve a teaspoonful of carbonate of soda in it, one pound of flour, two teaspoonfuls of cream of tartar rubbed well in the flour, and a little essence of lemon; mix all well together, and bake in a quick oven.

A FINE COWLEDGE, OR WEDDING CAKE.—Wash two and a half pounds of fresh butter in spring water first, then in rose water, beat the butter to a cream; beat twenty eggs, yolks and whites separately, half an hour; have ready two pounds and a half of the finest flour, well dried and kept hot, a pound and a half of sifted sugar, one ounce of spices, in fine powder, three pounds of currants, nicely cleaned and dry, half a pound of blanched almonds, three-quarters of a pound of citron, mixed with orange and lemon; let all be kept by the fire; mix all the dry ingredients in by degrees; beat them thoroughly; then add a half pound of stoned raisins, chopped as fine as possible, so that there are no lumps, and a teacupful of orange flower water; beat it all together for one hour; have a good sized cake tin, well buttered; take a white paper, doubled, and put it round the edge of the cake tin; it should not be more than three parts full, as there must be space allowed for rising. It will take from three to four hours' baking.

ROUT DROP CAKES.—Mix two pounds of flour into one of butter, one of sugar, one of currants, clean and dry; then wet into a stiff paste with two eggs, a large spoonful of orange flower water, and a spoonful of brandy; drop on a tin plate, floured. They will require a very short time to bake.

BUTTER CAKES.—Take a pound and a half of flour, one pound of butter, two eggs, one ounce of cinnamon, one rind of lemon-peel, grated, one pound of brown or white sugar, with a little essence of almond or lemon, two ounces of ground rice, and a little ginger; mix all together, and make into a stiff paste, roll out thin, and cut with either shapes, a glass, or top of flour dredge. Bake in a hot oven for ten minutes. Add a pinch of salt to all cakes and sweets.

A GOOD POUND CAKE.—Take one pound of flour, well dried and sifted, eight eggs, yolks and whites well beaten separately; then beat one pound of good fresh butter to a cream; add one pound of sifted sugar to the butter; beat for ten minutes until it gets to a cream; then add the eggs to it, with a little essence of almonds, and the grated rind of a lemon, no spices, a little salt; then mix the flour very slowly to the eggs, butter and sugar; a few ground almonds is a great improvement; beat for one hour, and bake in a brisk oven. Be sure to note the way it is directed.

BOLA.—Mix a pound and a half of flour with four egg, two good spoonfuls of yeast, and three-quarters of a pound of good fresh butter; make it into a dough; let it rise for three or four hours, then knead and roll out; then spread thinly cut citron, cinnamon, nutmeg, and finely chopped almonds over the top; roll it all up, and cut into two inch pieces; bake in a tin pan; when baked in a quick oven, put some good thick clarified syrup over them; insert the clarified sugar with a knife.

A CHEAP SEED CAKE.—Mix a pound and a half of flour with half a pound of sugar, some allspice, a little ginger, and some seeds; melt three-quarters of a pound of butter, in half a pint of milk; when just warm add to it a quarter of a pint of yeast, and work it up to a good dough; let it stand before the fire a few minutes before it goes in the oven. Bake an hour and a half. Milk by itself causes cakes and bread to dry soon.

QUEEN CAKES.—Mix a pound of dried flour with a pound of sifted sugar and some currants; wash a pound of butter in some rose water; beat it well, then mix with it eight eggs, yolks and whites, separately; put in the dry ingredients by degrees; beat the whole an hour; butter little tins, teacups, or saucers; have them only half full with the batter, and bake. Sift a little fine sugar over as you place them in the oven

GROUND RICE CAKE.—Mix half a pound of ground rice, half a pound of sifted sugar, with two ounces of ground cinnamon, the yolks eight eggs, and the whites of six eggs, beaten to a snow, the grated rind of a lemon; beat them well together for one hour.

A NICE CAKE FOR A CORNER DISH.—Use the same ingredients as in ground rice cake. When it is a day old, cut it round, and spread each slice with different kinds of preserves, and place them again in their places; blanch and split some almonds; stick them on the top of the cake, so as to look like a porcupine; strew sifted sugar on the top.

WHITE POUND CAKE, OR SILVER CAKE.—Take the whites of twelve eggs, five cups of flour, one cup of sugar, one cup of butter, one cup of cream, one teaspoonful of cream of tartar, half a teaspoonful of carbonate of soda, and salt; beat the butter and sugar together; add the rind of a lemon, grated, with a little essence of peach kernels; beat all together for three-quarters of an hour.

SPONGE CAKE.—Weigh ten eggs, and their weight in very fine sugar, and the weight of six eggs in flour; beat the yolks with the flour; rub the sugar first in the flour, and beat the whites to a snow; then by degrees add the ingredients to the whites, and beat it well for half an hour. This cake can be baked in a flat tin, and when cold it may be spread with a preserve, rolled up and cut as a luncheon with white sugar over it.

CUP CAKE.—Three cups of sugar, two cups of butter, five cups of flour, one pound of currants, one cup of milk, five eggs, and one teaspoonful of soda; mix the ingredients all together first; add these to the milk, eggs, and butter, with some nutmeg and a pinch of salt.

DROP CAKES.—Five cups of flour, three of sugar, one of butter, one of cream, half a teaspoonful of saleratus, and two eggs; lay small rings in a baking tin, well buttered, and drop the cakes in each ring.

TEA CAKES.—Rub two teaspoonfuls of cream of tartar and two tablespoonfuls of white sugar in one quart of flour, add two eggs, well beaten, and a piece of melted butter, the size of an egg; mix all together with one pint of milk and one teaspoonful of soda dissolved in a little milk; bake them in muffin rings. To be eaten hot.

LEMON CAKE.—One cup of butter, three cups of white powdered sugar, four cups of flour, five eggs, one cup of milk, one teaspoonful of soda, and one grated lemon; mix all together, and bake in a quick oven.

JELLY CAKE.—One and a half cups of sugar, two and a half of flour, half a cup of butter, one of milk, one egg, one spoonful of soda, and two of cream of tartar; bake in thin cakes, and spread currant or any other jelly over the top of each while it is hot.

MUSH CAKES.—Take a quart of cold mush, half a pint of wheaten flour, and a little salt; mix them in a little butter; make it into cakes, flour them, and bake on a griddle, or in an oven.

KRULLERS.—Two cups of sugar, one of sour milk, four eggs, four tablespoonfuls of butter, and one teaspoonful of saleratus dissolved in milk; after it is well mixed with sufficient flour to form a dough, let it stand an hour. To be fried in either oil or butter.

MATRIMONY CAKES.—Make a rich puff paste, (see directions in pastry receipts,) roll it out very thin, spread some currants, a little sugar, cinnamon, nutmeg, and a little candied peel, cut very small; cover it with the rest of the paste; strew sugar on top, and bake in a quick oven.

A TIPSY CAKE.—Put a sponge cake into a deep glass dish, pour round it some white wine, and a glassful of brandy, and some sifted sugar; let the wine soak in the cake; then pour over it a rich, thick custard. Ornament the top of the cake by sticking a light flower in the centre, or bits of clear jelly, then split some sweet almonds and strew them thickly over the cake.

BRIDE CAKE.—One pound of butter, one pound of pulverized sugar, beat them together with the hand; then add by degrees twelve eggs, well beaten, one pound of flour, three pounds of currants, well washed, picked, and dried, two pounds of best raisins, stoned, one pound of citron, half a pound of candied lemon-peel, one pound of blanched almonds, one cupful of syrup, one cupful of brandy, half an ounce of mace; cloves, cinnamon, nutmeg, and spices to suit. Bake five hours.

DOUGH NUTS, No. 1.—Rub a quarter of a pound of butter into a pound of flour; then add five ounces of sugar, two eggs, about a dessert spoonful of yeast, and sufficient milk to make it into a stiff paste; let it stand to rise; then roll it out and cut into shapes; fry them either in butter or oil till they are a nice brown.

DOUGH NUTS, No. 2.—Take half a pound of butter, a quarter of a pound of sugar, one pint and a half of milk; beat two eggs with the sugar, add half a pint of good yeast; flavor it with cinnamon and grated nutmeg; let it rise; when it has risen sufficiently, roll it out in squares, and fry in butter or oil; turn them often in the pan; when they are sufficiently brown, turn them out, and lay them on a cloth to drain the grease from them; then place them on a dish, and sprinkle powdered sugar over them.

SALLY LUNN CAKES.—Take three pounds of flour, one quart of milk, half a pound of butter, four eggs, well beaten, one tablespoonful of sugar, a cupful of yeast, and a little salt; mix them well together; when they have risen, bake them three-quarters of an hour.

GINGER BREAD.—Mix with two pounds of flour half a pound of molasses, three-quarters of an ounce of caraway seeds, one ounce of grated ginger, half a pound of butter. Roll the paste into what form you please, and bake it on tins; after it has risen well, candied peel, grated nutmeg, allspice, and cinnamon may be added, which will improve it.

SOFT GINGER BREAD.—Take one cup and a half of molasses, one cup of brown sugar, two ounces of butter, beat up five eggs separately, one tablespoonful of ground ginger, a teaspoonful of soda, and as much flour as will thicken it to the consistency of a pound cake; butter your pan, add citron and caraway seed; mix all well together, and bake in a hot oven.

GINGER SNAPS.—Two cups of molasses, one cup of butter, a tablespoonful of ground ginger, half a pound of flour, one teaspoonful of saleratus; mix all together, and roll out thin. Bake in a hot oven. One egg may be added.

JUMBLES.—Roll half a pound of butter with half a pound of flour, half a pound of sugar, one egg, wet with a little milk; roll out very thin, and cut into a round shape. Use plenty of ground ginger.

SUET WAFERS.—Take two ounces of butter, half a pound of sugar, half a pound of flour, five eggs, well beaten separately; then mix the ingredients all together; bake them in well greased wafer irons over the fire, and roll them over a knife.

WAFERS.—Dry the flour well, mix a little pounded sugar and a little ground mace together, then make it into a thick batter, with cream; butter the wafer irons, let them be hot; put a teaspoonful of the batter into them, bake carefully, and roll them off the iron with a stick.

SCOTCH SHORT BREAD, No. 1.—Mix two pounds of sifted flour with a pound of powdered sugar, three ounces of candied peel, cut small, a half pound of caraway comfits, and a pinch of salt; mix these with half a pound of butter, melted; then make the paste, roll it out the thickness of half an inch, cut into cakes, place them on tins, prick them, and bake a pale color.

Short bread may be made the same way.

SCOTCH BREAD CAKE, No. 2.—Take one pound and a quarter of flour, one pound of butter, one pound of sugar, and three eggs; mix them together; use no water; roll out, and bake on a square; when nearly baked, take out and place sugar comfits on top, and then finish baking.

SPANISH CHARLOTTE.—Place some stale cake on the bottom of your mould, on which put some tart apples, or any other acid fruit; lay a layer over your cake; continue this alternately until the dish is nearly full, making the cake form the top; pour a custard over it, and bake. Serve with a sauce of sweetened cream, or butter and sugar flavored with wine.

MACAROONS.—Four ounces of ground almonds, pounded, and four spoonfuls of orange flower water; whisk the whites of four eggs to a snow, then mix one pound of sifted sugar, with the almonds, to a paste; lay a sheet of wafer paper on a tin, and put it on in different cakes the shape of macaroons.

COCOANUT MACAROONS.—To one grated cocoanut add its weight in sugar, and the white of one egg, beaten to a snow; stir it well, and cook a little; then wet your hands and mould it into small oval cakes; grease a paper and lay them on; bake in a gentle oven.

A GOOD PLAIN BUN.—Mix one pound and a half of dried flour with a half pound of sugar; melt a pound of butter in a little warm water, add six spoonfuls of rose water, and knead the above into a light dough, with half a pint of yeast, then mix five ounces of caraway comfit seeds in, and put some on the outside.

TO PREPARE FOR ICING.—The white of one egg dissolved with a small quantity of gum arabic; wet the cake with it, and be careful to put them smoothly into the mould, using a broad knife for the purpose of levelling the top. For flavoring, essence of almonds is best.

ALMOND ICING FOR WEDDING CAKES.—Beat the whites of three eggs to a snow, two pounds of ground almonds in two teaspoonfuls of rose water; mix them lightly together with the eggs; put in by degrees a pound of loaf sugar, in powder; when the cake is baked enough, take it out and lay on the icing; then put it in a very cool oven to harden.

ICING FOR WEDDING CAKES.—Two pounds of the very best finely powdered sugar, the whites of eggs sufficient to make a stiff paste, mix together as much cream of tartar as will lie on a dime; beat all together for thirty minutes. When the cake is cold, spread with a knife, and bake in a very gentle oven; be careful that it does not brown.

KRAPFEN, OR GERMAN PUFFS.—Take half a pound of flour, five ounces of butter, three eggs, half a gill of cream, one ounce of sugar, half an ounce of German yeast, the grated rind of two lemons and one orange; then set the sponge with one-fourth part of the flour and the yeast and let it rise in a warm place, then spread out the flour in the form of a ring, and put the sugar, salt, butter, eggs and cream in the centre; work it all well together with both hands; rub the paste quickly about on the board, then gather it all up together and throw it down on the board with force; repeat this for five minutes, as soon as the sponge has risen enough let it be added to the paste and well mixed with it; then gather up the krapfen and place it in a clean napkin, covered with flour, to prevent the paste sticking, set it in a cool place to rise; this will take about four hours; knead the paste, then place it again in a cool place for half an hour; let it be cut up in about fifteen pieces, knead these in the form of balls; then put them in rows of four on separate sheets of paper, greased with butter; then put them on baking tins and set them to rise in a warm place; when they have risen then fry them a light color; as soon as they are done, drain them on a napkin and strew cinnamon, orange and sugar on the top; dish them up in a pyramid form on a napkin, and serve them with some preserves, or with clarified sugar.

DAMPFNUDELN, OR GERMAN DUMPLINS.—They are made with the same kind of paste as the krapfen. When it has fermented properly lay it on the pastry board, knead it into a dozen small rolls, then put them in a preserving pan about an inch apart; pour as much milk over them as will cover them, and as soon as they have risen twice their size put them in the oven and bake them a light color; before taking them from the oven see that the milk is not all soaked; then glaze them over with white sugar and a red hot salamander; dish them up on a napkin, and serve with vanilla sauce in a sauce boat.

GERMAN KOUGLAUFF.—Take one pound of flour, half a pound and two ounces of butter, four eggs, three-quarters of an ounce of German yeast, two ounces of sugar, quarter of an ounce of ground cinnamon, one grated lemon-peel, quarter of an ounce of salt, quarter of a pint of cream, and three ounces of ground almonds; put the butter in a large sized pan and work it well with a wooden spoon for ten minutes, so that it will look like cream, then add the cinnamon, lemon and pounded sugar, about one half of the flour and two eggs; work it all quickly together for a few minutes, then add the remainder of the flour and eggs gradually, continuing to work the paste with the wooden spoon; when it all has been used up spread out the paste in the middle and add the yeast, which has been dissolved in the cream and salt made luke-warm for the purpose; work the whole well; then pour this batter in a mould, greased well with butter; split the almonds and put them round the mould close together; bake it in a moderate oven; it must be a nice yellow color when done; strew some cinnamon and sugar over the cake. Bolas can be made from this paste, by rolling it out and spreading candied peel, ground almonds, sugar and cinnamon inside; cut into three inch slips.

POTATO SOUFFLE, FOR PASSOVER.—Take six ounces of potato flour, ten ounces of sifted sugar, four ounces of butter, one pint of cream, twelve eggs, some flavoring of vanilla, and a little salt, boil the cream or milk, then put in the vanilla, place the lid on the saucepan and let it stand for an hour; next put the potato flour, the sugar, butter, a pinch of salt, and one egg, into a preserving pan; mix all together; then add the milk and vanilla and stir the whole together on the fire until it boils, when it must be worked with a spoon to make it smooth; then add the yolks of the ten eggs, put them aside until the ten whites are whipped to a fine snow, add these to the souffle batter; pour the whole of it in a souffle dish with a broad band of paper round the outside, and then put it in the oven; it will take from three-quarters of an hour to an hour to bake; it must be dished up very hot; remove the paper bands, strew some sifted sugar over it, and serve quickly.

Souffle can be made with flour, ground rice, semolina, arrow root, or tapioca, and can be flavored with any kind of essence in the same way as above.

CROQUANTE OF ORANGES.—Remove the peel and pith of about one dozen oranges, not over ripe, then divide them in small pieces; do not break the thin skin which contains the juicy pulp; then put them on an earthenware dish; put one pound of the best lump sugar into a preserving pan, with sufficient water to cover it, and boil it down until it snaps; try it in the following manner: take up a little of the sugar, when it begins to boil in large bubbles, on the point of a knife, and quickly dip it into cold water; if the sugar becomes set, it is done, and will then easily snap in breaking. When boiling sugar for this purpose, put in a pinch of cream of tartar and calcined alum, mixed, or a few drops of acetic acid. The sugar should now be taken from the fire; the pieces of orange, stuck on small wooden skewers, should be slightly dipped in the sugar, and fixed at the bottom and around the sides of a plain, round mould, greased with the best salad oil; when it is done, and the sugar firm by cooling, before it is sent to table, fill the inside of the croquante with whipped cream, sugar, and some whole strawberries, and then turn out on a napkin and serve.

CORN OYSTERS.—Take six ears of boiled corn, three eggs, a tablespoonful and a half of flour; beat the yolks well, until they are thick; grate the corn off the cobs, and season it with pepper and salt; mix it with the yolks and add the flour; whisk the whites to a stiff froth; stir them in the corn and yolks; put a spoonful of the batter at a time in a pan of hot butter, and fry a light brown on both sides.

SHORT PASTE FOR TARTS.—Take one pound of flour, half a pound of butter, two ounces of ground sugar, a pinch of salt, two eggs, and about a gill of water; make a hole in the centre of the flour, then add the sugar, butter, salt, and water; break in the two eggs, and work it well together into a firm paste; it can be used for tartlets. If for a meat dinner, melted fat may be substituted for the butter.

ARROW ROOT LEMON JELLY.—Mix three tablespoonfuls of arrow root in enough cold water to form a paste; add a pint and a half of boiling water; stir it quickly; boil a few minutes; then add the juice and rind of two lemons, half a pound of sugar, cinnamon, or nutmeg.

PUDDINGS.

Observations on Puddings.

Be sure that the cloth is thoroughly clean, or it will make the pudding taste badly; it should be dipped in hot water, squeezed dry and floured when used. If bread pudding, it should be tied loose; if batter, tied tightly. The water should boil quick when the pudding is put in, and it should be moved about for a minute, lest the ingredients should not mix. Batter pudding should be strained though a coarse sieve. The ingredients must all be mixed first, then add the eggs, mixed separately. All utensils must be well greased.

A BAKED PUDDING (STHEPHON) OF RIPE FRUIT OR APPLES.—Half a pound of suet, not melted fat, chopped fine, with three-quarters of a pound of flour, a pinch of salt, not more flour than that quantity, as it will make it heavy; it is better to use equal quantities of flour and fat, and make a dough with sufficient water; when well mixed with the fat, etc., roll out thin and put flour on it, and then roll up and beat it hard with a rolling pin four or five times; cut it to the shape of the brown pan, and fill it in with some stewed fruit in different layers, until all is in the pan; bake in a moderate oven for three hours; when nearly done, take the yolk of an egg, or wet with water, strew sugar thickly over it, and bake for ten minutes, or until the sugar on top is brown. Apples and grocers' currants will make a good sthephon. To be turned out on a dish large enough to hold the juice. All boiled puddings are best when made with suet. Germans use a great deal of goose fat in their cooking.

A LUXION.—Take three eggs and one pound of flour, make up into a paste, roll out into very thin cakes, let them dry, and cut into strips one inch and a half wide, and boil for ten minutes; then pour them off, and place in cold water for five minutes; strain through a colander; then prepare eight eggs, well beaten, and half a pound of stoned raisins, one-quarter of a pound of sugar, two ounces of candied peel, a few ground almonds, one-quarter of a pound of chopped suet, one-quarter of a pound of currants, a little ginger, cinnamon and nutmeg; put some ginger in the frimsels and a pinch of salt, mix all together with the frimsels; grease a pan well, fill it, and bake in a hot oven. It can be made with butter and milk for a butter dinner. Fat should be used if for a meat dinner.

BAKED ALMOND PUDDING.—One pound of ground almonds and seventeen eggs, beat the whites and yolks separately, then add to the eggs well beaten together one pound of white sifted sugar, then put the almonds in lightly with the grated rind of a lemon, a little orange flower water, or vanilla, or essence of lemon, and beat for one hour; grease the dishes with sweet oil if for a meat dinner, and bake half an hour in a quick oven, try with a straw. To be eaten when cold; strew a little sugar over the top; clarified sugar may be added to them after they are baked, a pound will fill six small dishes; be sure not to fill the dishes too full, as it will waste; when made properly they will be very light. Beat the eggs first, separately, in all puddings.

BREAD AND BUTTER PUDDING.—Cut some bread in thin slices and butter, lay them in a dish with currants, citron, orange or lemon, a few almonds, and the grated rind of orange peel in layers; make a custard of one quart of milk, with cinnamon, nutmeg, vanilla, or any flavoring that is preferred, add to it eight eggs, well beaten, and four ounces of white sugar, lay it over the bread at least two hours before baking; it can be eaten either hot or cold; a light puff paste around the dish will improve it.

A GOOD LEMON PUDDING.—Beat the yolks of four eggs, add four ounces of white sugar, the rind of one lemon being rubbed with some lumps of sugar to take the essence, then peal and beat it in a mortar with the juice of a large lemon, and mix all with four or five ounces of butter warmed; put a good puff crust into a shallow dish and nick the edges, then pour in the ingredients and bake.

A VERY FINE AMBER PUDDING.—Melt a pound of butter in a saucepan, then add three-quarters of a pound of white sugar, finely powdered, then add the yolks of fifteen eggs, well beaten, and as much candied orange peel or lemon as will give color and flavor to it, being first beaten to a fine paste; line the dish with paste for turning out, and when filled with the above, lay a crust over as you would a pie, and bake in a slow oven. It is as good cold as hot.

YORKSHIRE PUDDING.—Mix a quarter of a pound of flour with a quart of water, (or milk, if for supper,) and three eggs, well beaten; grease the pan; when brown, turn the other side upward and brown that; it should be made in a square pan, and cut into pieces to send to table.

FRESH FRUIT PUDDINGS.—Make a paste with three-quarters of a pound of flour, and three-quarters of a pound of chopped suet and a pinch of salt; add enough water to make a light paste; line a basin with the paste, fill it up with the fruit and sugar; cover it with the paste; then flour a cloth that has been dipped in hot water and tie it close and tight, boil till the fruit is tender; turn it out of the basin and send it to the table; be careful not to break it.

CUMBERLAND PUDDING.—Mix six ounces of grated bread, the same quantity of currants, well cleaned, six ounces of chopped suet, six ounces of chopped apples, some lump sugar, six eggs, some nutmeg, pinch of salt, a grated lemon peel; mix it thoroughly, and put in a basin; cover very close with floured cloths, and boil three hours. Serve it with pudding sauce and the juice of half a lemon, boiled together.

IRISH POTATO PUDDING.—(*One that will do for Passover.*)—Boil six large potatoes in their skins; let them remain till next day, then peel them and grate on a horseradish-grater very light; then beat up six eggs, separately, the whites to a snow; add six ounces of sifted sugar, a pinch of salt, two ounces of ground almonds, and the grated rind of a lemon; beat all lightly together, and bake or steam in a mould with four ounces of melted fat.

FIG PUDDING.—Three-quarters of a pound of grated bread crumbs, half a pound of chopped suet, half a pound of fresh figs, chopped, six ounces of brown sugar, a little cinnamon, nutmeg and six eggs; boil in a mould. To be eaten with some sauce; if made for a butter supper, one pint of milk and one egg may be used.

RICE PUDDING.—Soak four ounces of rice in warm water, half an hour, drain the latter from it, and throw it in a stewpan with half a pint of milk, half a stick of cinnamon, and simmer till tender. When cold, add four eggs, well beaten, two ounces of butter, melted, in a teacupful of cream, three ounces of sugar, some nutmeg, and a good sized piece of lemon peel Put a light puff paste, or grated rusks, into a mould or dish, and bake in a quick oven.

A RICE PUDDING, No. 2.—Boil half a pound of rice in water, and a little salt, till tender; drain it dry; mix with it the whites and yolks of four eggs, separately, four ounces of chopped suet, three-quarters of a pound of currants, two spoonfuls of brandy, one of peach water or essence of almonds, nutmeg, and one lemon peel, grated. When well mixed, put a puff paste round the dish; bake in a moderate oven. For supper, substitute butter and cream for suet.

RICE PUDDING, No. 3.—Put into a very deep pan four or six ounces of rice, two ounces of butter, four ounces of sugar, a little nutmeg, and two quarts of milk. Bake in a slow oven.

BRANDY PUDDING.—Line a mould with stoned raisins or dried cherries, then with some slices of light bread, next to which put some ratifias or macaroons in layers until the mould be full, sprinkling in at times two glasses of brandy. Beat four eggs, yolks and whites, put to it a pint of milk, slightly sweetened, a little nutmeg, and the rind of a lemon, grated. Let the liquid sink into the solid part, then flour a cloth and tie it tightly over; boil for one hour; keep the mould right side up. Serve with pudding sauce.

SWEET POTATO PUDDING.—Beat half a pound of butter with half a pound of white sifted sugar, very light, a pinch of salt, and separate the yolks of five eggs, beat lightly and whisk the whites to a snow, the juice and rind of one lemon, one tablespoonful of brandy, a teaspoonful of rose water; then add all together and beat lightly. Line two tin plates with a rich puff paste, and bake a nice brown. When done and cool, sift white sugar over it.

GOOSEBERRY BISCUIT PUDDING.—Take a quart of gooseberries, and boil them in very little water with some sugar, according to liking; when tender mash them through a sieve; beat the yolks of three eggs with one ounce of very fine bread crumbs; beat to a snow the whites of three eggs with two ounces of white sugar, and put it on top of the dish with the gooseberries beaten smoothly; bake in a gentle oven for ten or fifteen minutes, with a light paste around the dish.

TRANSPARENT PUDDING.—Beat eight eggs briskly, put them in the stewpan with half a pound of powdered sugar, the same quantity of butter, and a little nutmeg. Set in on the fire, and keep stirring till it thickens, then set it into a basin to cool; put a rich puff paste around the edge of the dish, pour in your pudding, and bake it in a moderate oven. You may add candied orange and citron if you like.

CABINET PUDDING.—Grease the inside of a mould with good sweet butter, and ornament the sides with seedless raisins and candied peel; fill the mould with alternate layers of sponge cake and ratifias or macaroons; then fill up the mould with a lemon custard made with five eggs, one pint of milk, six ounces of white sugar, a glass of brandy, and the grated rind of a lemon; mix it up. Steam the pudding in a saucepan of hot water, not too full, so that the water does not reach the mould; it will take one hour and a half to steam. Dish up with a sweet sauce or custard.

BAKED POTATO PUDDING.—Take half a pound of butter, half a pound of sugar, grate one pound of cold boiled potatoes, add two ounces of ground almonds, a little rose water, or whatever essence is preferred, and six eggs; beat the butter and sugar to a cream, then add the potatoes; beat the whites and yolks of the eggs separately, and add them to the other ingredients; bake it as soon as it is mixed.

TAPIOCA, OR SAGO PUDDING.—One pint of tapioca or sago, one quart of new milk, two eggs, a teaspoonful of salt, some grated nutmeg; soak the tapioca, then put it in the milk, set the dish containing them into a kettle of boiling water; the tapioca will become tender if boiled in this way; stir frequently during the boiling; it must boil till it is cooked and well mixed with the milk; then remove it from the fire, beat the eggs, to which add sugar according to taste, stir them in the pudding; pour all in the baking dish, buttered well; two tablespoonfuls of sweet cream, or half a teaspoonful of butter are added last; it should be flavored with vanilla or with whatever essence is preferred; raisins or currants can be added; bake one hour; any sweet sauce may be used.

FARINA PUDDING.—Four spoonfuls of farina, two quarts of milk, two eggs, well beaten, sugar to taste; mix the farina with one quart of the cold milk, and boil the other, set it away to get cool, then mix all in a mould together, and bake for one hour.

CARROT PUDDING, No. 1.—Take six ounces of bread crumbs, two ounces of lemon peel, six ounces of white sugar, six ounces of chopped suet, six ounces of grated carrots, six ounces of ground almonds, a little nutmeg, four eggs all beaten well together, and flavored with either orange flower water or essence of lemon; to be steamed over a saucepan of boiling water for one hour and a half. To be eaten with a wine sauce, made as in directions for sauces. In making sauces be sure never to boil the egg, but add the boiling gravy to it, as it will prevent its curdling. Grease the moulds well before using them.

CARROT PUDDING, No. 2.—Half a pound of grated carrot, half a pound of chopped suet, half a pound of flour, some cinnamon, nutmeg, a pinch of salt, half a pound of raisins and two ounces of citron. To be steamed for five hours. A pinch of salt should be used in all sweet things.

HOMINY PUDDING.—Take one pint of hominy and boil in a quart of milk, six ounces of white sugar, six ounces of butter, six eggs, some grated nutmeg, one gill of wine, a little grated lemon peel; bake for an hour in a dish.

CAKE PUDDING.—Cut some stale sponge cake into slices, and put a layer of it in a mould, then a layer of either citron, raisins and currants, mixed, or any kind of jam or jelly, or apples thinly sliced, then another layer of cake; then pour over it a custard, made of a quart of milk, eight eggs, and three ounces of sugar. It does not require to be too sweet, as the cake or fruit will be sweet enough. Flavor it with vanilla or essence of almonds. Stale rusks can be used for this pudding. Bake in a moderate oven; serve it with wine sauce.

APPLE PUDDING, No. 1.—Take one pound of sifted our, one pound of chopped suet, a pinch of salt; rub the suet into the flour until it is smooth; then make a dough with water, not too stiff, and beat it well with a rolling pin, so as to get the fat smooth and light; roll out three times, and sprinkle flour each time you roll it, and beat it; then have ready some good cooking apples, pared, cored, and cut up in slices, with the rind of a lemon, grated, sugar, cinnamon, and cloves. Line your basin with dough, rolled out rather thin, and place the apples inside, with a pint of water, and cover it over with the paste; scald a thick cloth and tie it up tight; have a saucepan with water boiling, and a plate at the bottom. Boil for three hours, taking care not to let it stop boiling as that will make it heavy. When done untie the cloth and turn it out of the basin, and send it to table hot.

APPLE PUDDING, No. 2.—Butter a pie dish well, and cover the bottom and sides with grated bread crumbs, very thickly; press them on, then nearly fill the dish with good sour apples, previously stewed and flavored with cinnamon, nutmeg, grated lemon peel, and the juice of one lemon. Cover it over with bread crumbs again, and lay over it pieces of butter; bake it slowly for half an hour, and dish up with a sweet sauce.

CHARLESTON PUDDING.—Beat six eggs separately, then add three-quarters of a pound of sugar to the yolks; make a cream of four cups of flour, one of butter and one of sweet milk; rub a teaspoonful of soda in the flour smoothly; then dissolve two teaspoonfuls of cream of tartar in a wineglassful of water; add lastly the whites, beaten to a snow; beat up the other ingredients well before adding the whites, then stir in the whites lightly; do not beat it up after the whites are in; bake in a moderate oven; when it is done, turn it out and sift powdered sugar over it. To be eaten with a sweet sauce.

YEAST DUMPLINGS.—Take a piece of very light bread dough, and make it into small dumplings, boil in a saucepan with some boiling water for twenty minutes; eat with butter, sugar, and lemon juice or molasses; to be eaten hot, as they become heavy in their steam; tear them apart with two forks.

SUET DUMPLINGS.—Chop half a pound of suet, mix with half a pound of flour, a teaspoonful of salt, and water; make a dough, not too stiff; they can be boiled with salt meat or in plain water, and eaten whilst hot. Suet is always best for boiled pastry, as it makes it lighter. Use equal quantities of flour and fat.

A RICH (PUREEM) PUDDING.—(*Feast of Esther.*)—For a moderate sized one: take one pound of currants, one pound of raisins, one pound of sugar, one pound of suet chopped very fine, half a pound of bread crumbs, half a pound of flour, quarter of a pound of almonds, half a pound of mixed candied peel, a nutmeg, a teaspoonful of ginger, and a pinch of salt; rub all these ingredients together first, as it will make it lighter; then add fourteen eggs, well beaten, whites and yolks separately, and beat till thoroughly mixed. Have ready a large saucepan of boiling water, with a plate at the bottom; add to the pudding a good glass of brandy, and place all in a mould, or cloth tied, so as to leave room for swelling, but not too loose. Lift it from the boiling water two or three times, then leave it to boil for three or four hours; dish it with lighted brandy and blanched almonds on top, taking care that the dish is perfectly dry before setting fire to the brandy; dish up also with a sauce, made as follows: beat up two eggs, whites and yolks separately, with a teaspoonful of hot water to prevent curdling; put a tumblerful of wine to the eggs; do not boil either, but have ready a teaspoonful of flour and half a pint of water boiled with two ounces of sugar, one lemon rind and juice. When well boiled add it to the wine and eggs; stir gently and it will not curdle; some add a few ground almonds.

GROUND ALMOND PUDDING, BOILED.—Take half a pound of ground almonds, half a pound of white sifted sugar, eight eggs, the whites and yolks beaten separately, half a pound of bread crumbs, and the rind of one lemon; beaten for half an hour, and steamed the same as carrot pudding. Must be dished up quickly, and eaten with a sauce.

Marrow Pudding may be made the same as above, only add half a pound of marrow, and make the same way.

Lemon Pudding—Make in the same manner as above, only add the grated rind of a lemon and the juice.

BOILED RASPBERRY AND CURRANT PUDDING.—Make a paste with three-quarters of a pound of flour, three-quarters of a pound of chopped suet, and sufficient water to make a light paste; add a pinch of salt; line a mould or basin with the paste, and fill it with raspberries and currants, then cover the top with the paste; dip a cloth in boiling water and flour it, then tie the pudding very tight, so that water will not get in; let it boil for two or three hours; when dishing be careful not to break it; be sure not to roll the paste too thin nor too thick.

PLAIN BREAD PUDDING.—Take eight ounces of grated bread crumbs, six ounces of sugar, for butter four ounces, for meat four ounces of chopped suet, the rind of a lemon, three yolks of eggs, and two whites whipped to a snow, and a pinch of salt. If for butter, put the ingredients into a basin with the eggs; pour over a pint of boiling milk; cover it up and let it soak for about fifteen minutes, then add the eggs to it. Mix the whole well together; pour this preparation into a well-greased mould, and steam it for an hour, and when done dish it up with some arrow root sauce, made in this way: mix a teaspoonful of arrow root with two tablespoonfuls of white sugar, the juice of one lemon, a little nutmeg, and a cup of water; stir it over the fire until it boils. It can be made the same for a meat dinner, only leaving out the butter and milk, and substituting fat and water.

CHOCOLATE PUDDING.—Take one cup of sweet chocolate, one cup of grated crackers, one cup of sugar, and five eggs; beat the whites to a snow, and the yolks well beaten; then beat them all together for half an hour, and grease the tins well; bake in a hot oven.

STEWED PRUNES WITH BALLS.—Put two pounds of prunes in a saucepan with half a pound of sugar, some cinnamon, nutmeg, allspice, a pinch of salt, add the rind of a lemon; make some balls of two eggs, four ounces of bread crumbs, and two ounces of ground almonds; mix all together and roll into balls with one ounce of chopped suet, and one ounce of sugar, and boil for ten minutes. Dish up hot or cold.

BATTER PUDDING WITH MILK.—Rub three spoonfuls of flour very smooth, by degrees, into a pint of milk; simmer till it thickens; stir in two ounces of butter, and set it to cool; then add the yolks of three eggs. Flour a cloth that has been dipped in hot water, or butter a basin and put the batter in it. If put in a bag, tie it tight, and plunge it into boiling water, the bottom upwards; boil it for an hour and a half. Serve with plain butter or sweet sauce.

A PUDDING SAUCE, *(to keep for years.)*—Take half a pint of noyau, a pint of good sherry, the rind of four or five lemons, pared very thin, and a little mace. Mix all together and let it stand for two or three weeks; then strain it, and add a pint of very strong syrup of curacoa. Bottle it up; it is excellent for several dishes, but chiefly for puddings, added to melted butter.

MATZAS CHARLOTTE, *(unleavened bread for supper.)*—Soak about three matzas (cakes) in cold water; when tender, strain them dry on a sieve by laying each piece separately; have ready some butter and some stoned raisins, grated peel, nutmeg, cinnamon, and sugar; lay the pieces on a dish in layers, and put the fruit on with a good custard, prepared in this way: one quart of milk and seven eggs, well beaten with four ounces of white sugar, and a stick of cinnamon.

COMMON PANCAKES.—Make a light batter of eggs and milk, fry in a small frying pan in hot oil or butter when made with milk; but if with water, they may be fried in fat.

GOOD PANCAKES.—Beat six eggs well, the whites separately; mix them with half a pint of cream, four ounces of sugar, a glass of wine, a little nutmeg, stir in a quarter of a pound of butter, just warmed, add as much flour as will make a batter thick enough; fry in as little butter as possible; can be eaten with jelly or jam.

BAKED APPLE PUDDING.—(*For a supper dish.*) Grate a pound of apples, and add half a pound of sweet butter, half a pound of white sugar, the yolks of six eggs, the whites of three eggs beaten separately, the peel of one lemon, grated, and the juice of half a lemon; mix all well together, and put it into a dish with a puff paste around it.

DATE PUDDING.—Chop up a pound of dates, a pound of bread crumbs, half a pound of chopped suet, a pinch of salt, half a pound of sugar, and a little nutmeg and cinnamon; mix all together with four eggs, well beaten; steam it in a mould for three hours.

A fig pudding may be made the same way.

JAM ROLY POLY PUDDING.—Make a crust as in directions of boiled pastry; roll it out rather thin; spread any jam over it, and leave space at the ends; roll it round and tie it in a well floured cloth; put it in boiling water; it will take two hours to cook.

PEAS PUDDING.—Soak a quart of split peas over night, then tie them loosely in a cloth and put them into a saucepan of cold soft water for about two hours and a half; when the peas are tender, drain them and rub them through a colander with a wooden spoon; stir in some butter, or if for a meat dinner, use fat, pepper, salt and one egg; then tie it tight in a cloth, and boil it another hour; turn it out on a dish, and serve it hot with salt beef.

GATEAU DE POMMES.—Boil one pound of sugar in a pint of water until the water evaporates; then add two pounds of apples, pared and cored, the juice and grated peel of a lemon; boil all together till quite stiff, then put it in a mould, and when it is cold serve with custard around it.

CHARLOTTE RUSSE.—Weigh ten eggs, and add their weight in very fine sugar, and the weight of six eggs in flour; beat the yolks with the flour; rub the sugar first in the flour, and beat the whites to a snow; then by degrees add the ingredients to the whites, and beat it well for half an hour. The cake can be baked on a flat tin; when cold, cut in thin slices and line a mould with it; soak one ounce of gelatine with a pint of milk for one hour; it must be cold; put it on the fire, and keep stirring until dissolved; take it from the fire and beat well with an egg-beater; then flavor with a quart of cream, a teaspoonful of extract of vanilla, and a wineglassful of brandy; sweeten to taste; mix all together, beat thoroughly and fill the moulds that have been previously lined with the cake, and put away, either on ice or in a cool place, until needed.

RICE FLUMMERY.—Boil in a pint of milk a piece of lemon peel and a stick of cinnamon; mix with it a little cold milk and as much ground rice as will make the whole of a good consistency; sweeten, and add a spoonful of peach water, or essence of almonds; boil it, observing not to burn it; pour it into a mould, taking out the spices; when cold, turn the flummery into a dish and serve with cream, milk or custard.

BLANC-MANGE.—Boil two ounces of gelatine, or isinglass, in one pint and a half of water, half an hour; strain and sweeten it; add some flavoring, such as essence of almonds, etc.; let it boil but once and put it into some nice moulds; if you do not wish it too stiff, use less isinglass; let the blanc-mange settle before you turn it into moulds, or the black will remain at the bottom of them and be on the top of the blanc-mange when taken out of the moulds.

LEMON SAUCE.—Rub and roll half a dozen good sized lemons in order to get the juice easily; take out the seeds; put to it two tablespoonfuls of fresh grated horseradish, two tablespoonfuls of ground ginger, one tablespoonful of mace and cinnamon, and one grated nutmeg; add a pint of the best vinegar; scald it for ten minutes. When it is cold, strain it off and bottle. Used to flavor piquant sauces.

GRIMSLECHS. (פסח *For Passover.*)—Chop up half a pound of stoned raisins and almonds, with half a dozen apples and half a pound of currants, half a pound of brown sugar, nutmeg, cinnamon, half a pound of fat, the rind of a lemon, two soaked matzas or unleavened bread; mix all the ingredients together with four well beaten eggs; do not stiffen too much with the matzo meal; make into oval shapes; either fry in fat, or bake in an oven a light brown.

MATZO FRITTERS. (*For Passover.*)—Take some soaked unleavened cakes and beat them up with three or four eggs, lightly, add a pinch of salt, and fry in oil or fat, a light brown. Meal can be used the same way. To be eaten with stewed fruit.

MISS P. LAFETRA'S PUDDING.—Stew half a dozen apples until tender, then season with sugar, cinnamon, cloves and grated lemon peel and nutmeg; then prepare a mould with some stale pound cake or sponge cake, grated; line the basin with the grated cake crumbs, put in alternately layers of apple and cake, with a few lumps of butter; when the basin is half full pour over a rich boiled custard, and serve with wine sauce.

PASTRY.

Observations on Pastry.

Any smart cook will be careful to have the board nice and clean before making her pastry, and will not leave any of the dough adhering to the pan or board while making. It is best when rolled on marble. In very hot weather the butter should be put into cold water, to keep it as firm as possible; and if made early in the morning to be preserved from the air until it is baked. A good pastry cook will use less butter and make lighter crusts than others.

Using preserved fruits in pastry.—Preserved fruits should never be baked long; those that have been prepared with their full proportion of sugar need no baking; the crust should be baked in a tin shape, and a bit of bread put in to keep them in shape; when baked, take out the bread and add the preserve. It can be baked in small dishes, or tart pans, in fanciful shapes, such as cross bars or leaves.

How to keep suet for a year.—Take the firmest parts and pick free from skin and veins; put it in a saucepan of water and boil it; it is better not to melt it in a frying pan, as it will taste; when boiled let it cool off, then strain it and wipe it dry; fold it in fine paper and put it in a linen bag; keep it in a dry but not hot place. When used, scrape it fine, and it will make a fine crust.

A RICH CRUST FOR CHEESECAKES OR PRESERVES.—Take a pound of the best flour, well dried; mix with it three ounces of refined sugar, then work half a pound of butter in it with your hand till it comes to a froth; put the flour into it by degrees, and work into it, well beaten and strained, the yolks of three and the whites of two eggs; if too limber, put in some flour and sugar to make it fit to roll. Line your small pans and fill; a little over fifteen minutes will bake them. When they are done, have ready some refined sugar beaten up with the white of an egg as thick as you can. Ice them all over; set them in an oven to harden, and serve cold. Use fresh butter.

MERINGUES.—Half a pound of sifted sugar and six eggs; whisk the whites in a large pan until they are perfectly white and thick like snow; then take a spoon and mix in the sugar lightly; do not work it too much, as it will make it soft, and it will be difficult to make the meringue. They can be shaped better when the batter is firm. Cut some foolscap paper into bands about two inches wide; then take a spoon nearly full of the batter, working it up at the side of the bowl in the form of an egg, and drop this slopingly upon one of the bands of the paper, at the same time drawing the edge of the spoon sharply around the outer base of the meringue, so as to give it a smooth and rounded appearance, that it may resemble an egg; do it all in the same way until the band is full; keep the meringues about two inches apart on the paper; as the bands are filled place them close beside each other on the table, and when the batter is used up shake some rather coarse sugar all over them and let it remain for three or four minutes; then take hold of one of the bands at each end, clear off the loose sugar; place the meringues on the board, allowing sufficient room for the oven, and so on with all the rest; bake a light color in a slow oven;

when done, each piece of meringue must be carefully removed from the paper, the white part inside scooped out with a dessert spoon, and nicely smoothed over; they must then be placed in order on a baking sheet and put back into the oven to dry; take care they do not get more color. Previous to sending the meringues to table, whip some good cream with a little sifted sugar, a glass of brandy, a few drops of orange flower water, or vanilla; garnish each with a teaspoonful of this cream; join two together, dish them up in a pyramidal form on a napkin; you can make them all sizes to vary their form or appearance; previous to shaking the sugar over them, strew over them some fine pounded pestachios, or almonds, rough granite sugar, colored preserves, or any kind of ice creams.

MINCE PIE, WITHOUT MEAT.—Take six pounds of good apples, pared, cored, and minced; three pounds of fresh suet, or butter, and raisins stoned and minced; to these add a quarter of a ounce of mace, cinnamon, eight cloves in powder, three pounds of white sugar, a little salt, the rinds of four and the juice of two lemons, half a pint of port wine, and the same of brandy; mix well and put into a deep pan. Have washed and dried four pounds of currants, and add one pound of citron on candied peel.

A LIGHT PUFF PASTE.—It can never be made as nicely in summer as in cold weather, unless you are well supplied with ice; the butter must be kept in ice water until it is firm; mix it in a cool kitchen and use ice water to wet the flour; do not handle it more than you can possibly help; after it is mixed set it away in a pan, cover it with a cloth, and set it on ice; sift one pound of flour, reserve one-quarter of a pound;

work out all the buttermilk from the butter; divide it into four equal parts, rub one-fourth of it into the flour, until it is smooth, wet this into a smooth dough, a little stiff, with a half a pint of water, a teaspoonful of salt, dissolved, then divide the rest of the butter into six parts; roll out half an inch thick, then place one of the parts of the butter rolled to the size of the paste; then sprinkle this with the other quarter of a pound of flour, fold it twice and turn it so the points will be towards you; flour the rolling-pin, and press it evenly and lightly and roll it from you, an inch thick; take care not to let the butter burst through the paste; repeat this until all the butter is used up; keep it as cool as possible; after it has been rolled each time put it away on ice for a quarter of an hour longer; if convenient, when the dough is finished, put it away on ice for two or three hours; then wet small pieces large enough for the size of your tart; use just enough flour to prevent it sticking to the slab or rolling-pin; you must use judgment in wetting the flour.

A RICH PUFF PASTE.—Take equal quantities of flour and butter as will be necessary for what you want; mix a little butter with the flour, and wet it with as much water as will make it into a stiff paste. Roll it out, and put half the butter over it in slices, turn the ends in and roll it thin; do this twice, and touch it as little as possible. It requires a quicker oven than for short crust. Set it away for three hours before making it into tarts.

RICE PASTE.—For those who do not like flour paste, boil a quarter of a pound of rice in the smallest quantity of water; strain from it all the moisture as well as you can; beat it in a mortar with either half a pound of butter or fat, and one egg, well beaten, and it will make an excellent paste for tarts, etc.

GERMAN PUFFS.—Boil sixteen tablespoonfuls of flour in a quart of milk, and a little salt, then add to it six eggs; stir until fine; then butter twelve baking cups, and bake in a heated oven. To be eaten with clarified sugar, made in the following manner: take half a pint of water, half a pound of loaf sugar, and the rind of a lemon. Boil for twenty minutes. I would recommend less salt in all sweet things.

CHEESE PUFFS.—Take half a pint of cheese curd, strain well, a teaspoonful and a half of flour, three eggs, leave out the whites of two, a teaspoonful of orange flower water, a little nutmeg, and two ounces of white sugar; beat it fine; lay it in little patty pans, lined with puff paste. Bake in a hot oven a quarter of an hour.

ICING FOR TARTS.—Beat the white of an egg to a snow; wash the paste with it, and sift white sugar thickly on the top, after the paste has been baked, and then return it to the oven; bake in a gentle oven till it is iced.

RHUBARB FOR TARTS.—Cut the rhubard into pieces of three or four inches long, and, with a little water and sugar to sweeten, or a thin syrup, stew one hour; then make a light paste, and line the dish with the paste.

COCOANUT TARTS.—After taking off the brown skin, grate the cocoanut fine, then mix three ounces of powdered white sugar with it; grate the rind of a lemon, and with the milk of the cocoanut make a nice paste. Line some tin baking dishes with a puff paste, and put the mixture into them. Bake a nice brown color.

LEMON TARTS.—Squeeze two large lemons and grate the rinds, strain the juice, and add two ounces of ground almonds, two ounces of grated bread crumbs, two ounces of suet or fat, six eggs, yolks and whites beaten separately to a snow, with four ounces of sifted sugar. Make a light puff paste around the dish, and bake in a quick oven.

COCOANUT CHEESECAKES.—Take the milk and grate the cocoanut without the brown skin, put it with its weight of white sugar into a saucepan, perfectly clean and tinned; keep gently stirring it until it is tender; it will take an hour to make it so; when it is cooled off, then add six eggs, the whites beaten to a froth, the yolks beaten separately, and the rind of a lemon, grated. Line some patty pans with a puff paste, and put in the mixture. Bake a quarter of an hour in a good hot oven.

A PLAIN CHEESECAKE.—Turn three quarts of milk to curd, break it and drain off the whey; when dry break it into a pan with two ounces of butter, beat till perfectly smooth; add to it a pint and a half of thin cream or good milk, and add sugar, cinnamon, nutmeg, and three ounces of currants.

SUGAR COOKIES, No. 1.—One and a half cups of sugar, one egg, half a cup of butter, half a cup of sweet milk, one teaspoonful of soda, and two teaspoonfuls of cream of tartar; roll and bake on buttered tins.

SUGAR COOKIES, No. 2.—Take one cup of sugar, half a cup of butter, one egg, and one-quarter of a teaspoonful of soda; roll very thin.

STICKIES.—Make a pastry, as before directed in pastry recipe, and cut into shapes; double them over as large as three inches long and square, and have prepared one pound of brown sugar, and half a pound of butter, boiling hot in a frying pan. Fry the stickies in this, and turn them over two or three times till they are well candied. They can be eaten hot or cold.

LEMON CHEESECAKES.—Mix four ounces of sifted lump sugar, and four ounces of melted butter; then add the yolks of two eggs and white of one, the rind of three lemons, grated fine, and the juice of one and a half. Half a pound of ladies'-finger biscuits, a few ground almonds, and a spoonful of brandy; mix well; put a light puff paste around the dish, and bake in a quick oven.

Orange cheesecakes are made in the same way, only the peel must be boiled in two or three waters, to take out the bitterness.

STRAWBERRY SHORTCAKE.—Take half a cup of butter, one quart of flour, one quart of milk, one teaspoonful of soda, and make into a dough; roll it out thin and bake it. When done split it, and spread with butter and fresh strawberries.

AN EXCELLENT TRIFLE.—Lay macaroons and ratafia over the bottom of a glass trifle dish, and pour some port wine over the cakes; pour over this some cold, rich custard; it must be two or three inches thick; on this put a layer of raspberry jam, and cover the whole with a very high whip of rich cream, made the day before, the whites of two eggs beaten to a snow, and grated lemon peel. Some prefer it made the day before, as it is thicker and far better. Very small candies, such as hundreds and thousands, strewed on top, will make it look beautiful for company.

GOOSEBERRY FOOL.—Put a quart of gooseberries into an earthenware lined saucepan with a little water at the bottom; when it is done enough to pulp, press it through a colander; have ready, if for supper, a cupful of cream and fresh milk boiled together, or three eggs instead of milk, well beaten; the fruit must be added to the raw egg whilst it is hot; sweeten and strew some cinnamon on the top; it is best eaten cold.

Rhubarb can be prepared in the same way, or cut into small pieces, and stewed in a syrup of white sugar, made in this way: a pint of water and one pound of sugar.

LAMPLECHS.—Take some light puff paste, roll it out and strew over chopped raisins, currants, apples, nutmeg, cinnamon and ground almonds; cut the paste into three inch lengths, and cover it with the same, and strew thickly over white sugar; first wet the paste on the top with a brush using the white of a beaten egg or water, and bake in a quick oven a light brown.

CHARLOTTE DE POMMES.—Butter a plain mould, and line it with thin slices of stale bread, dipped in clarified butter, joining each slice neatly, to prevent the syrup from escaping, which would spoil the appearance of the charlotte when done; then fill the mould with apple marmalade and apricot jam; cover the top with slices of bread dipped in butter, and on the top of the bread put a plate with a weight on it; set the mould in a quick oven from three-quarters of an hour to one hour, according to the size; turn it out with care, having drained the butter from it before taking it from the mould; sift loaf sugar over it, or cover it with clear jelly, and serve it hot.

PRESERVES, JELLIES, ETC.

TO CLARIFY SUGAR FOR SWEETMEATS.—Break as much sugar as you may require in large lumps, and put a pound to a half a pint of water, in a bowl, and dissolve. Set it on the fire with the white of an egg, well whipped; let it boil up, and when ready to boil over, pour a little cold water in it to stop it; when it rises a second time, take it off the fire, and set it by in a pan for a quarter of an hour, during which time the foulness will sink to the bottom, and leave a black scum on the top; which take off with a skimmer, and pour the syrup into a vessel quickly from the sediment.

TO PRESERVE PEACHES, No. 1.—When ripe, choose the yellow ones, pare them as thin as possible, and weigh them; lay them in halves on dishes, the hollow part upwards; have ready an equal weight of good lump sugar, pounded, and strew it over them; when the fruit has lain twelve hours, put it with the sugar and juice into a preserving pan; let it simmer very gently till clear, then take out the pieces of peaches singly, put them into small pots on tins, and pour the syrup over them; the scum must be taken off as it rises. Cover them with white paper dipped in brandy.

TO PRESERVE PEACHES, No. 2.—Peel them a good round shape, take a quarter of a pound of white sugar to every pound of peaches; boil the peaches for fifteen minutes to make the syrup. You can preserve all fruits in the same way; be sure to bottle them air tight, as they will spoil if the air gets at them.

TO PRESERVE GREEN PLUMS.—Take the largest when they are ripe, and strew over them an equal quantity of sugar, which has been weighed; next day pour the syrup from the fruit, and boil it with the remainder of the sugar for six or eight minutes, very gently; skin and add the plums; some persons like to use the kernels; simmer till clear, taking off any skum that rises; put the fruit singly into pots, and pour the syrup over it.

TO PRESERVE WHOLE OR HALF QUINCES.—In two quarts of water put a quantity of good juicy apples cut in thick slices, not pared but wiped very clean; boil them very quickly, till the water becomes a thick jelly, then scald the quinces. To every pint of pippin jelly put a pound of the finest sugar; boil and skim it clear. Put those quinces that are to be done whole in the syrup at once, and let it boil fast; and those that are to be in halves by themselves; skim it and when the fruit is clear, put some of the syrup into a plate to try if it jellies, before taking off the fire. The quantity of quinces is to be a pound to a pound of sugar and a pound of jelly, already boiled with sugar.

TO PRESERVE FRUITS FOR WINTER USE.—It is necessary to observe that the boiling of sugar constitutes, more or less, the chief art of the confectioner, and those who are not practised in this, and preserve only for family use, are not aware that in two or three minutes a syrup over the fire will pass from one grade to another, known by the confectioner as degrees of boiling, of which there are several. Underboiling prevents sweetmeats from keeping, while quick and continued boiling brings them to a candy.

Preserves should be kept in a very dry place,

otherwise they may ferment or become mouldy. They should be looked at two or three times in the first two months, that they may be gently boiled again if necessary.

Attention, without much practice, will enable a person to preserve any of the following kinds of sweetmeats, etc., and they embrace nearly all that are needed in a private family; the finer preserved fruits can be purchased for less than it costs to put them up yourself. Jellies of fruit, made with equal quantities of sugar, that is a pound to a pint, require but slight boiling.

TO PRESERVE FRUIT FOR FAMILY DESSERTS.—Gather cherries or plums of any sort, and American apples, when ripe, lay them in small jars that will hold a pound; strew over each jar six ounces of loaf sugar, pounded; cover with two bladders, each separately tied down; then set the jars in a stewpan of water, up to the neck, and let it boil gently for three hours. Keep these and all other kinds of fruit from damp.

ORANGE MARMALADE.—Cut out the pulp, then slice the rind and, boil very tender. Boil three pounds of white pounded sugar in a pint of water, skim it and add a pound of the rind; boil fast till the syrup is very thick, but stir it carefully; then put in the pulp and juice, (the seeds must be removed,) and a pint of apple liquor, if approved. Boil all gently until well jellied, which it will be in about half an hour.

Lemon Marmalade may be made in the same way.

They are fine sweetmeats. If these recipes are correctly followed out, they will prove very satisfactory.

QUINCE MARMALADE.—Pare and quarter quinces, weigh an equal quantity of sugar; to four pounds of the latter put a quart of water, boil and skim; then lay them in a stone jar, with a teacup of water at the bottom, and pack them with a little sugar strewed between; cover the jar close, set it on a stove or cool oven, and let them soften till the color is red; then pour the fruit, syrup, and a quart of quince juice into a preserving pan, and boil all together till the marmalade is completed; break the hard pieces. This fruit is so hard it requires a great deal of time.

APPLE MARMALADE.—Scald apples till they will pulp from the core; then take an equal weight of sugar in large lumps, dip them in water, add a little grated lemon peel, not too much, as it will make it bitter; and boil on a quick fire a quarter of an hour.

CHERRY JAM.—To each pound of cherries, weigh a pound of sugar; break the stones and blanch them; then put them to the fruit and sugar, and boil gently till the jam comes clear from the pan. Pour it into China plates and dry. Keep in boxes with white paper between.

CURRANT JAM, BLACK, RED, OR WHITE.—Let the fruit be very ripe, pick it clean from the stalks, bruise it; to every pound of fruit put three-quarters of a pound of loaf sugar; stir and skim it well; boil for two hours.

GOOSEBERRY JAM.—Take some nice large green gooseberries when ripe, put a pound of gooseberries to three-quarters of a pound of fine sugar, and half a pint of water; boil and skim the sugar and water, then put the fruit in, boil it gently till clear, then mash and put it into jars.

RASPBERRY JAM.—Take seven pounds of raspberries and six pounds of sugar. Put the former into a preserving pan; boil and break; stir constantly, and let it boil very gently. When the juice is almost wasted, add the sugar, and simmer half an hour; it is better to boil the fruit first and then add the sugar, as it preserves the color and flavor.

CURRANT JELLY, RED OR BLACK,—Strip the fruit, and put it in a stone jar; stew them in a saucepan of water, or by boiling it on the stove; strain off the liquor, and to every pint of liquor a pound of loaf sugar; when nearly dissolved add the sugar; then put it in a preserving pan. Simmer and skim as necessary. When it will jelly on a plate, put it in small jars or glasses, and put white paper steeped in good brandy on top.

CALF'S FEET JELLY.—Boil two feet in one quart and a pint of water, till tender, and the water is half wasted; strain it, and when cold, take off the fat; then put it in a saucepan with the juice and rind of two lemons, and some sugar; beat up the whites of five eggs to a snow; do not stir the jelly after it begins to warm. Let it boil twenty minutes after it rises to a head, then dip the jelly bag in hot water, and pour it through the bag, which must be made of flannel. Run it through and through until it is clear; then put it into moulds or jelly glasses. The best way to clear the jelly is to throw a teacupful of cold water in and let it boil five minutes, then take the saucepan off the fire, cover it closely for half an hour; it will only require one running through the bag. Flavor it highly with brandy or some good wine.

VARIEGATED JELLY.—One ounce of gelatine to one quart of boiling water, one-half pound of white sugar, the rind and juice of two good sized lemons, one-half pint of good wine, or two gills of brandy, a pinch of salt, the whites of two eggs, beaten to a snow; give one boil up and then strain through the flannel jelly bag. Orange, or any fruit or flavor may be substituted.

Prepare some jelly with gold and silver water; remove the skin from six ounces of pistachios, and cut each kernel into six strips; set a jelly mould in a large pan on some pounded ice, pour a little of the jelly into a mould; then place some of the prepared pistachios, or any other fruit, into it; when it has become firm, pour in more of the jelly and pistachios, as the layers become set; repeat the process until the mould is filled, and allow the jelly to remain on the ice long enough to congeal.

COLORINGS FOR JELLIES, ICES, OR CAKES.—*For Red*—Boil very slowly for half an hour fifteen grains of powdered cochineal and a drachm and a half of cream of tartar, in half a pint of water, add a piece of alum the size of a pea, or use beet root sliced, and some liquor poured over.

For White—Use almonds, finely powdered, with a little water or cream.

For Yellow—Yolks of eggs, or a bit of saffron steeped in the liquid and squeezed.

For Green—Pound spinach or beet leaves, press out the juice, and boil a teacupful in a saucepan of water, to take off the rawness.

APPLE JELLY.—Prepare twenty good sized apples; boil them in a pint and a half of water till quite soft;

then strain the juice through a colander; to every pint of liquor put three-quarters of a pound of sugar; add grated lemon or orange peel, and boil to a jelly.

HOW TO PREPARE ICE FOR CREAMS.—Break a few pounds of ice into small pieces, throw a handful of salt on, prepare in the coolest part of the cellar; the ice and salt being in a bucket, put your cream in an ice pot, cover it and steep it in the ice. In a few minutes put a spoon in it and stir well, removing the parts that ice round the edges to the centre; if the ice cream be in a form, shut the bottom close and move the whole in the ice; there should be holes in the bucket to let off the water as the ice melts.

ICE CREAMS.—Mix the juice of the fruits with as much sugar as will be wanted, before you add the cream, which should not be very rich.

LEMON CREAM.—Take a pint of thick cream, and add to it the yolks of two eggs, well beaten, four ounces of white sugar, and the thin rind of a lemon; boil it up; then stir it until almost cold. Put the juice of a lemon in a dish or bowl, and pour the cream upon it, stirring it till quite cold.

CHOCOLATE CREAM.—Scrape into one quart of thick cream one ounce of the best chocolate, and a quarter of a pound of sugar; boil it and mill it; when quite smooth take it off the fire and leave it to get cold; then add the whites of nine eggs, whisk and take up the froth in sieves; and serve the froth in glasses, to rise above some of the cream.

AN EXCELLENT CREAM.—Whip up three gills of cream to a strong froth with some finely grated lemon peel, a squeeze of the juice, half a glass of sweet wine and sugar to make it pleasant, but not too sweet; lay it on a sieve or in a mould; next day put it on a dish and ornament it with very light puff paste biscuit, made in tin moulds the length of a finger, and about two inches thick, over which sugar may be strewed, or a light glaze with isinglass, or you may use macaroons on the edge of the dish.

A CREAM FOR AN EVENING PARTY.—Boil half a pint of cream and half a pint of milk with a bay leaf, some lemon peel, a few ground almonds, sugar according to taste, and a little orange flower water; mix with the above a teaspoonful of flour made smooth with a little cold milk; when cold add a little lemon juice to the cream and serve it in cups or lemonade glasses.

FLOATING ISLAND.—One pint of cream and the whites of three eggs. Sweeten the cream to taste and add a gill of wine, if preferred; whisk the whites of the eggs to a dry froth and add a little lemon juice, orange flower water, or any essence. Let the cream boil up once, and then stir in the yolks of the eggs, which have first been beaten very light. Do not let the cream boil after putting in the eggs. Pile the froth upon the cream, and serve soon, as the whites will fall.

CURRANT OR RASPBERRY WATER ICE.—The juice of these, or any other sort of fruit, being gained by squeezing, sweetened and mixed with water, will be ready for icing.

LEMON DROPS.—Grate three large lemons, and a large piece of loaf sugar; then scrape the sugar into a plate, add half a teaspoonful of flour; mix well, and beat into a light paste with the white of an egg. Drop it upon white paper, and put them into a moderate oven, on a tin plate.

GINGER DROPS, GOOD FOR THE STOMACH.—Beat two ounces of fresh candied orange in a mortar, with a little sugar, to a paste; then mix one ounce of powdered white ginger with one pound of loaf sugar. Wet the sugar with a little water, and boil it together to a candy; drop it on paper the size or mint drops.

PEPPERMINT DROPS.—Pound and sift four ounces of refined sugar, beat it with the whites of two eggs, till perfectly smooth; then add sixty drops of oil of peppermint; beat it well, and drop on white paper, and dry at a distance from the fire.

RATAFIA DROPS.—Mix four ounces of ground almonds, with a little pounded or sifted sugar, then add the remainder of the sugar, and the whites of two eggs, beaten, making a paste; of which put little balls the size of a nutmeg, on wafer paper, and bake gently on tin plates.

TO KEEP DAMSONS FOR WINTER PIES.—Put the fruit in stone jars or wide-mouthed bottles, up to their necks in a saucepan of cold water; scald them; next day, when cold, fill up with water, and cover them; you can boil one-third as much sugar as fruit with it until the juice adheres to the fruit and forms a jam; the general proportion of sugar must be three pounds to nine pounds of fruit. When it is cold, put a clean stick into the middle of the jar and let the upper end stand above the top. Cover the fruit with white paper; then pour melted mutton suet over the top, half an inch thick. Keep the jars in a dry cool place.

HOW TO KEEP ORANGES, LEMONS, ETC.—Squeeze the fruit, and throw the outside in water, without the pulp. Let them remain in the same a fortnight, adding no more. Boil them therein till tender; strain it from them, and when they are tolerably dry, throw them into any jar or candy you may have remaining from old sweetmeats; or if you have none, boil a small quantity of syrup of white sugar and water and put over them. In a week or ten days boil them gently in it till they look clear, and that they may be covered in a jar with it. You may cut each half of the fruit in two.

ORANGE BUTTER.—Boil six eggs hard, beat them in a mortar with two ounces of fine sugar, three ounces of butter and two ounces of blanched ground almonds; moisten with orange flower water, and when well mixed rub it through a colander on a dish; serve it on sweet biscuits or crackers.

ORANGE CHIPS.—Cut oranges in halves, squeeze the juice through a sieve; soak the peel in water; next day boil in the same till tender; drain them and slice the peels; put them to the juice, weigh as much sugar and put all together into a broad earthen dish, and put over the fire at a moderate distance, stir it often till the chips candy; then set them in a cool room to dry. They will not be so under three weeks.

TO KEEP GRAPES, FRESH FROM THE VINE.—Gather fresh, ripe grapes, put them in a glass or stone jar, and seal them air tight; put them away in a dark, dry place

CHERRIES IN BRANDY.—Weigh the finest morellas, having cut off half the stalk; prick them and drop them in a jar or wide mouthed bottle. Strew over them three-quarters of the weight of sugar, fill up with brandy, and tie a bladder over.

SUGAR CANDY.—Take half a pint of water to one pound of white sugar, half a sheet of isinglass, and a teaspoonful of gum arabic; dissolve the whole in a preserving pan; when it commences to boil, take it from off the fire and skim it well; then put it on again and boil it until it is brittle; you can ascertain this by dropping a little in cold water; if it is made of white sugar, add a teaspoonful of vinegar, or it will be too brittle; flavor it with any essence you wish; it can be colored; if nuts, or any sweetmeats are put in, it should be done before pouring out the compound. It can be moulded to any shape.

TO CANDY ANY SORT OF FRUIT.—When finished in the syrup, put a layer into a new sieve and dip it suddenly into hot water to take off the syrup that hangs about it; put it on a napkin before the fire to drain, and then put some more in the sieve; have ready sifted double refined sugar, which sift over the fruit on all sides till quite white; set it on the shallow end of a sieve in a slightly warmed oven, and turn it two or three times. It must not be cold till dry. Watch it carefully and it will be beautiful.

HOW TO DRY CHERRIES.—To every five pounds of cherries stoned, weigh one of double refined sugar. Put the fruit into the preserving pan with very little water; make both scalding hot. Take the fruit immediately out and dry them; put them into the pan again, strewing the sugar between each layer of cherries; let it stand to melt, then set the pan on the fire and make it scalding hot, as before; take it off, and repeat this three times with the sugar. Drain them from the syrup, and lay them singly to dry on dishes, in the sun or on a stove. When dry, put them on a sieve, dip it into a pan of cold water, and draw it instantly out again, and pour them on a fine soft cloth. Dry them, and set them once more in the hot sun, or on a stove. Keep them in a box, with layers of white paper, in a dry place. This way is the best to give plumpness to the fruit, as well as color and flavor.

EXCELLENT SWEETMEATS.—Divide two pounds of peaches or apricots when just ripe, and take out the stones and break them, add the kernels without the skins to the fruit; add to it three pounds of greengages and two pounds and a half of lump sugar; simmer until the fruit is a clear jam; the sugar should be broken in large pieces and dipped in water, and added to the fruit over a slow fire; observe that it does not boil, and skim it well. If the sugar be clarified it will make the jam better.

STEWED PEARS.—Prepare some nice large hard stewing pears by peeling them very thin, and put them in a stewpan with water; cover well with brown sugar, cinnamon, grated lemon peel, whole ginger, grated nutmeg and whole allspice. Do not open the cover more than is necessary, and stew for five or six hours; when done, take them out and pour the liquor over them.

BAKED APPLES.—Take off a slice from the stalk end of some fine, large apples, and core, but do not pare them; mix some currants, grated lemon peel, almonds, chopped fine, and some candied peel, with some cinnamon, cloves and grated nutmeg. Make holes in the apples with a fork, and insert the spices, put them in a baking pan with plenty of brown sugar and a pint of water or raisin wine. Bake in a gentle oven.

MERINGUE CUSTARD.—Make a pastry of rich puff paste, as in directions for pastry, and line some tin plates with it; make a custard with eight well beaten eggs and one quart of new milk, flavored with vanilla, or any essence that is preferred, a grated lemon and six ounces of white sugar; grate the peel on some lumps of sugar; boil the milk for the custard with whole cinnamon, grated nutmeg and sugar; when it is cooled off a little add the milk to the eggs and beat all up together; line the plates with the custard, and bake for half an hour; when they are done, beat up the whites of four eggs to a thick snow, and two ounces of pulverized sugar; spread the snow over the custard pies about an inch thick, and bake a very light brown for two or three minutes. Any fruit tarts can be prepared the same way.

ORANGE TARTLETS.—Take out the pulp of two Seville oranges, and boil the peels until quite tender, then beat them to a paste with twice their weight in sifted white sugar; then add the pulp and juice of the oranges with a small piece of butter, and beat it all together; line some small patty pans with rich puff paste; lay the mixture in them, and bake for half an hour.

ROCK CAKES.—Rub half a pound of butter into a pound of dried flour and half a pound of fine moist sugar; mix this with two well beaten eggs, and half a glass of brandy or white wine, and a little essence of lemon; drop them on a baking sheet, and bake them for half an hour.

DRIED APPLES —Take some tart apples and put them in a cool oven six or seven times, and flatten them gently by degrees, when soft enough to bear it; the oven should be very cool at first; if too hot they will waste.

STEWED SMALL APPLES.—Core and pare the apples very fine, and throw them in cold water. For each pound of apples, mix half a pound of refined sugar in syrup with a pint of cold water; skim, and put in the apples; stew until clear; add a little grated lemon peel; do not let the apples break. This makes a fine dish for dessert.

DIET FOR INVALIDS.

Food for the Sick.

The following pages contain the principal food necessary for a sick person, as they are not able to take their usual nourishment. It may be necessary to advise what is best to agree with the patient, that a change be provided; that something is always prepared, and not too much at once. All invalids require a change in their food, and it should be made in different shapes and with varied flavors.

A VERY NOURISHING BROTH.—Put the knuckle of a leg of veal or shoulder, an old fowl, a piece of mutton, some mace, ginger, salt, a piece of bread, an onion if liked, and three quarts of water, into a stew-pan, and cover close; simmer slowly and skim it well, then strain and take off the fat. It will take four hours' boiling.

CALF'S FEET BROTH.—Put two feet in two quarts of water, and boil it to one half. When it is to be used take off the fat, put a large cupful of the jelly into the saucepan with half a glass of wine, a little sugar and nutmeg, and beat it up till it is ready to boil; then take a little of it and beat by degrees to the yolk of an egg; stir all together, but do not let it boil.

CHICKEN BROTH.—Take a chicken with a little rice, and put them in a saucepan with a quart of water, a little mace, ginger and salt, and let it boil till tender, add an onion, if preferred; take off the fat.

BEEF TEA.—Chop a pound of beef clear from any fat; put it in an earthenware pan or jar, and place it in a saucepan of boiling water till the juice comes out of the meat in the jar; then season with a little salt and ginger. It will take from two to three hours' boiling.

SAGO.—Soak it in cold water, to prevent its tasting earthy; pour that off, and wash it well; then add more, and simmer gently, till the berries are clear, with lemon peel and spices, if approved; add wine and sugar, and boil all together.

A FLOUR CAUDLE.—Into five large spoonfuls of the purest water rub one dessertspoonful of fine flour. Set over the fire five spoonfuls of new milk, and put two bits of sugar into it. The moment it boils, pour into it the flour and water, and stir it over a slow fire twenty minutes. It is a nourishing and astringent food.

RICE CAUDLE.—Take a quarter of a pound of rice, place it in a quart of water and boil it tender, then add some sugar, lemon peel, cinnamon, and a glass of brandy. Boil all smooth.

CAUDLE OR GRUEL.—Boil up half a pint of fine gruel with a bit of butter the size of a walnut, a little brandy, a spoonful of white wine, a bit of lemon peel, and nutmeg, if liked.

PANADA, MADE IN FIVE MINUTES.—Set a little water on the fire, add a glass of white wine, some sugar, a scrape of nutmeg and lemon peel, and some grated bread crumbs. The moment the mixture boils up, keeping it still on the fire, put the crumbs in, and let it boil as fast as it can. When of a proper thickness to drink, take it off.

SIPPETS, (*When the stomach refuses meat.*)—Put two or three sippets of bread on a very hot plate, and pour over them some gravy from beef, mutton, or veal. Sprinkle a little salt over them.

ARROWROOT JELLY.—Be sure to get the pure sort; if good it is very nourishing, especially for weak bowels. Put into a saucepan half a pint of water, a glass of sherry or a spoonful of the best brandy, grated nutmeg and sugar. Boil once up, then mix it by degrees, into a dessertspoonful of arrowroot, rubbed smooth, with a spoonful of cold water; then return the whole into the saucepan; stir and boil it three minutes.

TAPIOCA JELLY.—Choose the largest sort; pour cold water on to wash it two or three times; then soak it in fresh water five or six hours, and simmer it in the same until it becomes quite clear; then add lemon juice, wine, and sugar. The peel should have been boiled in it. It thickens very much.

Drinks for the Sick and Convalescent.

A REFRESHING DRINK, IN A FEVER.—Put a little sage, two sprigs of balm, and wood sorrel into a stone pitcher; they must be washed and dried; peel thinly a lemon, slice it and put a bit of the peel in; then pour in three pints of boiling water, sweeten and cover close.

A PLEASANT DRINK.—Wash well an ounce of pearl barley; sift it twice, then put to it three pints of water, an ounce of sweet almonds, beaten fine, and a bit of lemon peel; boil it till smooth, then put in a little syrup of lemons and capillaire.

BARLEY WATER.—Wash a cupful of common barley, then simmer it gently in three pints of water with a bit of lemon peel; add a little sugar. This is better than pearl barley, as it is less apt to nauseate.

TOAST WATER.—Toast slowly a thin piece of bread till well browned, but not the least blackened; then plunge it in a jug of cold water, and cover it over an hour before used. This is good for weak bowels.

A PLEASANT DRAUGHT.—Boil a quarter of an ounce of isinglass shavings with a pint of new milk to one half, add a bit of sugar, and, for a change, a bitter almond. It is best at bed time, not too warm.

MEDICINAL RECIPES.

Sickness may occur in every family, when the services of a physician cannot be had immediately; something must be done in the meantime, while waiting for the doctor. I trust some of these recipes will answer the purpose of temporary relief, while waiting for the doctor. Much sickness can be relieved without the aid of a physician by simple remedies, if taken in time. Experience and judgment must be exercised in the administration.

Caution in visiting the sick.—Do not visit a contagious sick room with an empty stomach, or when you feel fatigued, or when you are overcome with the heat and are perspiring, as in that state you are more liable to catch the disease, or impart it to others. When the disease is very contagious, take the side nearest the window, and wait till the room has been aired. When you leave the patient, take some food and change your clothing. Smoking is an excellent preventive to keep off the malaria.

For a bad smell in a sick room nothing is better than to burn green coffee. Fill a shovel with lighted coals, throw a handful of coffee on it, and pass it all over the room. Chloride of lime is also very good.

FAINTING.—Let the patient lay in a horizontal position, and have plenty of air; do not crowd around the patient in this condition; bathe the face with cold water and spirits of camphor; apply some stimulant to the nose, and loosen all the clothing; put mustard plasters on the extremities, if the patient does not revive quickly.

To relieve insensibility from a fall or blow on the head, bathe the head with hot vinegar, and apply a mustard poultice on the extremities.

FOR CONVULSIONS OR SPASMS.—Give some ipecac to cause vomiting; rub spirits of turpentine on the stomach; if from costiveness, give an injection of castor oil in water; if from teething, give paregoric and magnesia mixed, about half a teaspoonful. Mustard plasters on the spine and extremities may be applied; bathe the body in warm water; throw cold water on the head

DIPHTHERIA, No. 1.—In the early stages of the symptoms, accompanied by soreness and swelling of the throat, use a solution of salt and water, and gargle every ten minutes; have a large piece of flannel, double, wet it well with hot salt and water, and put salt between the folds of the flannel; bind this around the throat, and put a dry cloth outside; if the patient is much prostrated, use a stimulant, but do not lose any time before calling in a doctor.

DIPHTHERIA, No. 2.—Half a pint of strong sage tea, half a teaspoonful of alum, half a teaspoonful of pulverized borax, one tablespoonful of brewers' yeast, three tablespoonfuls of honey; then mix all together; for an adult, gargle; but for a child, let a small swab be made on a pencil or stick, pass it up and down the throat with care, so that it does not choke the child; be sure to have a clean swab each time it is applied, it can be made of linen; apply on the throat a piece of old rusty salt pork, and changed as often as possible.

SORE THROAT.—Make a gargle of salt and vinegar, it is good for a common sore throat.

One large spoonful of cayenne pepper, a teaspoonful of salt, and a pint of boiling water or half vinegar; pour on the water first, then add the vinegar; let it settle, and then gargle the throat every half hour. This is good for a putrid sore throat.

Bind on the throat a piece of salt pork, cut very thin, and if it is very bad keep it on two or three days; it will do it good.

A mustard poultice is also good.

Either of these are good for ulcerated sore throats.

Black currant jelly is a good remedy for sore throat or quinsy.

FOR CROUP. (*From a good Physician.*)—The whites of an egg beaten up with loaf sugar; give it to the child as often as possible.

CHILLS AND FEVER.—Take one blue pill before going to bed at night, a tablespoonful of castor oil in the morning; at least two hours before the attack comes on, take a strong tea of boneset and red pepper; keep the feet warm; a tea of corn shucks with morphine will sometimes prevent an attack. This remedy is much more preferable than quinine, as quinine will cause deafness by taking an over dose.

SCARLET FEVER.—As soon as the nature of the disease is known, rub the patient with fat bacon, night and morning, over every part of the body but the head; do it carefully.

LOCKJAW.—If caused by a wound, wash it well with arnica, diluted with water; bind a grated beet on it; rub around the wound, but not on it, with turpentine;

give ipecac in large doses to vomit, as this will relax the nerves; if the patient cannot take medicine, give an injection made of ipecac and laudanum, use a larger quantity than if it were taken in the mouth. Do not loose time to procure a doctor.

A GOOD AND SURE CURE FOR MEASLES.—When a doctor cannot be had in a hurry, take a peck of bran, put it into a wash kettle, and let it boil; make it like a thick poultice; put it into a washtub or bath; set the child in it as warm as it can bear it; then have ready another bath, with a quarter of a pound of saleratus in hot water; put the child immediately into it, and bathe it well; after which take it out quickly, and roll it in a woollen blanket; put it into bed, and keep it as warm as possible. Give to the child a drink of strong sage and saffron tea; the measles will be all out in twenty-four hours. Be sure to take care the child does not take cold, although the saleratus will prevent that.

HOW TO RELIEVE A COUGH.—Bathe the feet, before going to bed, with water as warm as can be borne, with a handful of salt and mustard in it; then take from three to five grains of quinine, and twenty drops of laudanum, in a tablespoonful of ginger tea. If the first dose does not relieve, repeat the next night. Two doses generally relieve an obstructed cold.

FOR COUGH AND COLDS.—One ounce of syrup, one of paregoric, and one of sweet spirits of nitre; boil some flaxseed, flavor it by boiling a lemon in it; sweeten with loaf sugar; if preferred, put a tablespoonful of the mixture into a wineglass, and take it when going to bed. Give it every three hours until relieved.

REFRESHING DRINK FOR A COUGH.—Beat a new laid egg, and mix with it a quarter of a pint of new milk, warmed, a large spoonful of capillaire, the same of rose water, and a little scraped nutmeg. Do not warm it after the egg is put in. Take it morning and evening.

AN EXCELLENT RECIPE FOR RHEUMATISM.—Take a pint of the best alcohol, and about two ounces of camphor; mix them both together, and let it stand closely corked for a week, then apply to the parts affected; it may be improved by adding one ounce of laudanum; it is also good for neuralgia. This remedy has never been known to fail.

CHOLERA MORBUS.—Take one teaspoonful of soda, one of cinnamon, and one of cloves; pour on them a pint of boiling water, and when nearly cold, add a large cupful of brandy, and sweeten with loaf sugar. Give a spoonful every half hour. If the disease is severe, give injections of castor oil and barley water.

A GOOD CURE FOR CHOLERA MORBUS.—Put two ounces of peppermint, two of spirits of camphor, two of laudanum, two of Hoffman's anodyne, one of extract of ginger, and two of red pepper. Mix all together, and take a tablespoonful every half hour.

USE OF GERMAN TEA.—This must be purchased at the German apothecaries, in packages; take two tablespoonfuls; let it steep in a teapot with a pint of boiling water, and stand on a stove for two hours. Dose: half a teacupful in the morning, fasting, and at bed time. It is good for costiveness, the blood, liver complaint, and bilious headache.

A PERFECT CURE FOR A FELON.—Soak the finger in weak lye; put it in cold, and sit near the fire till it scalds; make a poultice of the following: the yolk of an egg, six drops of turpentine, a few beet leaves, a little soap, a teaspoonful of burnt salt, and one of Indian meal. This is a sure remedy, if applied in time.

GOOD EFFECTS OF HOT WATER IN BRUISES.—Bathing the part with hot water prevents stiffness and black and blue marks; it is also good for removing pain. It must be applied as soon as possible, and as hot as it can be borne.

Soaking in hot water will cure a whitlow, if applied when the pain is first felt.

TREATMENT OF COLDS.—Bathe the feet in warm water; if feverish, take a glass of hot milk with a tablespoonful of the best whiskey and a tablespoonful of lime water, sweetened with sugar; and in the morning, fasting, one tablespoonful of castor oil in milk. Be careful about exposure next day.

ASTHMA.—Dip a sheet of brown paper in dissolved saltpetre, dry the paper, then burn a piece in a small room, and let the patient inhale the fumes.

CATARRH IN THE HEAD.—Snuff up fresh water ever night and morning; make a snuff of gum arabic, gum myrrh and bloodroot, pulverized. Wash the head and neck frequently. This disease sometimes ends in consumption.

A CURE FOR NAILS GROWING INTO THE FLESH.—Melt some tallow, and drop some between the nail and outside flesh. Be sure to see that the fat goes into all the parts under the nail. Do it often, if necessary.

TO CURE CORNS, No. 1.—Pare a lemon and cut it in thin slices, and place it on the corn for five or six nights, then in the morning soak the corn in strong common washing soda, the core then can be picked out.

TO CURE CORNS, No. 2.—Corns are caused by a tight shoe rubbing against the flesh. Put some sweet oil on it or them, after you have pared them with the tip of the finger, on getting up in the morning or on going to bed at night; the pain will diminish in a few days.

HOW TO CHECK BUNIONS.—When they first make their appearance rub on a bit of adhesive plaster, and keep it on as long as it feels painful; if it is inflamed, poultice it with bread and milk, and a little laudanum; easy shoes must be worn, or a piece cut out over the bunion; lard or spermacetti ointment should be rubbed on gently, two or three times a day.

FOR A COLD.—Make a good mustard poultice and apply to the chest, between two rags; put the feet in warm water, and wrap up in flannel; take a tumblerful of milk, a tablespoonful of good brandy or whiskey, a tablespoonful of lime water and some loaf sugar; take it when going to bed.

FROST-BITTEN LIMBS.—Bathe them immediately in cold water, and rub them until the circulation of the blood returns; do not warm them by the fire, as the sinews will draw up.

FOR FROSTED FEET.—Before they become open wounds, rub them every night with onion and salt, which allays the itching, or with lemon and salt.

FOR CHAPPED HANDS.—Rub them with lemon juice, or use glycerine.

CRAMP IN THE LEGS.—Stretch out the heel as far as possible, and at the same time draw the toes as much as possible towards the leg; it will give relief.

A GOOD REMEDY FOR SHORTNESS OF BREATH.—A teaspoonful of mustard in warm water; drink the water off; then take a teaspoonful of tincture of valerian every hour, until relieved, and apply a mustard poultice on the chest and back; soak the feet in warm water, lay in bed and keep warm. A little of Hoffman's drops may be used beneficially.

ASSAFŒTIDA.—This is an extremely useful medicine in flatulent nervous diseases, or to any one subject to hysteria, dyspepsia, or colic; to be given in doses of small pills, from the solid gum, in twenty grains. It must not be taken if there are any symptoms of in flammation. Families should never be without it in the house.

FOR A CUT.—To stop the blood apply some salt on the wound, hold the parts close together, and tie it up tightly; or pour in some good arnica or balsam, which good housekeepers should never be without.

SMELL OF THE BREATH BY ONIONS.—To prevent this eat the leaves of parsley dipped in vinegar.

BOILS.—They should be brought to a head by poulticing with warm onion root and poppy seeds, and fomentations of hot water; when ripe they should be opened with a needle, or the doctors' lance.

Milk of sulphur and molasses is very good to take, or Hamberger tea and sea bathing.

SALVE FOR BOILS.—The white of an egg, mixed with flour and honey.

HOW TO EXTINGUISH FIRE ON A PERSON.—If the clothes catch fire, put it out by wrapping woollen cloths around the person; take the rug or anything that is nearest, and smother it out. Never rush into the air. It may be extinguished by the persons throwing themselves on the floor and rolling over it.

FOR BLEEDING AT THE LUNGS.—Drink freely of strong salt and water every two or three minutes.

A CURE FOR CHILBLAINS OR FROSTED FEET.—Take five pounds of oak bark, and half a gallon of water; boil to a pint, and bathe the feet night and morning, in a wash bowl.

FOR MOSQUITO BITES.—Put into a glass or basin of cold water, one ounce of alum, a good handful of salt, and two tablespoonfuls of vinegar; rub it on at night, and let it dry in the flesh.

CHEESE, WINES, ETC.

TO MAKE CHEESE.—Put the milk into a large tub, warming a part until it is of a degree of heat nearly equal to new; if too hot the cheese will be tough. Put in as much rennet as will turn it, and cover it over. Let it stand until completely turned; then strike the curd down several times with the skimming dish, and let it separate, still keeping it covered. There are two modes of breaking the curd, and there will be a difference in the taste of the cheese accordingly as either is observed. One way is to gather the curd with the hands very gently towards the sides of the tub, letting the whey pass through the fingers until it is cleared, and skimming it off as it collects. The other mode is to get the whey from it by early breaking the curd. The last method deprives it of many of its oily particles, and is therefore less proper. Put the vat on a ladder over the tub, and fill it with the curd by the skimmer; press the curd close with your hand, and add more as it sinks; it must be left with two inches above the edge. Before filling the vat, lay the cheese cloth over the bottom, and when full, draw it smooth on all sides.

There are two modes of salting cheese; one way by mixing the salt with the curd while in the tub, after the whey is out, and the other is by putting the salt in the vat and crumbling the curd with it, after the first squeezing with the hands has dried it. The first method appears best on some accounts, but not on all, and, therefore, the custom of the country must direct. Put a board over, and one under the vat, and place it in the press. In two hours turn it out and put it in a fresh cloth; press it again for eight or nine hours; then salt it and turn it again in the vat; let it stand in the press for fourteen or fifteen hours, observing to put the cheese last made undermost. Before putting them the last time into the vat, pare the edges if they do not look smooth. The vat should have holes at the sides and at the bottom to allow the whey to pass through. Put on clean boards and change and scald them occasionally.

CREAM CHEESE, No. 1.—Put five quarts of new milk into a pan with five pints of cold and five pints of hot water, a little sugar, and as much rennet as will bring the whey in twenty minutes; when it comes strike the skimmer three or four times down and leave it on the curd. In an hour or two lade into the vat without touching it, and when the vat is full and the whey has run from it, put a weight upon it.

CREAM CHEESE, No. 2.—Take a pint of very thick sour cream from the top of the pan for gathering butter; lay a napkin on two plates and pour half of the cream into each plate. Let them stand twelve hours; then put them on a fresh wet napkin in one plate, and cover with the same. Do this every twelve hours until you find the cheese begins to look dry. It will be ready in ten days.

TO SCALD CREAM, (*as in the west of England.*)—In winter, let the milk stand twenty-four hours; in summer, twelve hours; then put the milkpan on a slow fire, or in a wide saucepan large enough to hold the pan; it must be on the fire till quite hot, but on no account boil, or there will be a skin instead of a cream upon the milk. You will know when it is done enough, as there will be a surface, looking thick and having a ring round the pan. The time allowed to scald cream depends on the size of the pan, and the heat of the fire; the slower the better. Remove the pan into the dairy when done, and skim it next day. In cold weather it may stand thirty-six hours, and never less than two meals. The butter is usually made of Devonshire cream this way, and if properly done it is very firm.

TO MAKE BUTTER.—In summer time skim the milk before the sun has heated the dairy; at this season it should stand, for butter, twenty-four hours without skimming, and forty-eight hours in winter; deposit the cream in a very cold cellar. If you cannot churn daily, change the cream into fresh scalded pots, but never omit churning twice a week. Keep the churn in the air, and if not a barrel one, set in a tub of water two feet deep, which will make the butter firm. When the butter is come, pour off the buttermilk and put the butter into a fresh scalded pan, or tubs which have been in cold water. Pour water on it, and let it lie to get hard before you work it. Then change the water and beat the butter with flat boards, so that not a particle of the buttermilk will remain; change the water until it ceases to become colored by the milk; then work some salt into the butter and make it into forms; put them into earthenware pans, filled with water, and cover them. You will then have very nice cool butter in the warmest weather.

TO PRESERVE BUTTER.—Take two parts of the best salt butter, one part of good loaf sugar, and one part of saltpetre; beat them well together. To sixteen ounces of butter, from which the buttermilk has been well worked, put one ounce of this composition; work it well, and when it has become firm and cold, pot it down. It should be kept from the air, in glazed pots, holding about fourteen pounds, and should not be used for a month at least.

TO PRESERVE BUTTER FOR WINTER.—When the butter has been prepared as above directed, take two parts of the best common salt, one part of good loaf sugar, one part of saltpetre, and beat well together. Work one ounce of this composition to sixteen ounces of butter; after the butter has become cold, press it into the pans, and put some salt on the top; if this does not make sufficient brine to cover the butter entirely, add some strong salt and water.

BLACK CURRANT WINE.—To every three quarts of juice put the same of water, and to every three quarts of the liquor add three pounds of good brown sugar. Put it into a cask, reserving a little for filling. Put the cask in a warm room, and the liquor will ferment of itself. Skim off the refuse, when the fermentation is over, and fill up with the reserved liquor. When it has ceased working pour three quarts of brandy to forty quarts of wine. Bung it close for nine months, then bottle it. Drain the thick part through a jelly bag until it is clear, and bottle that. Keep it ten or twelve months.

ORANGE WINE.—To five gallons of spring water put fifteen pounds of loaf sugar, and the whites of three eggs, well beaten; let it boil for half an hour, and as the scum rises take it off. When cold add the juice of sixty Seville oranges and five lemons; pare ten oranges and five lemons, as thin as possible, put them on thread, and suspend them in a barrel for two months; then take them out and put in a pound of loaf sugar, and bung up.

ELDERBERRY WINE.—Pour seven gallons of water over three gallons of berries; after it has stood two or three days, boil it an hour, and press the juice through a coarse cloth; then add to it fifteen pounds of sugar, half a pound of ginger, one ounce of cloves, one ounce of allspice. Boil all together, then put it in a tub, and when cold add some yeast, spread on toasted bread. After two days, put all in a cask, leaving the bung loose for two months; then add one quart of brandy.

CURRANT WINE.—To one quart of currant juice, add two quarts of water; as the currants that have been squeezed will still have some sourness left, put to them a pint more of water for every quart of juice which has been expressed; squeeze the currants again, and add the juice to the other liquid. Let it stand over night, then skim it, add fifteen pounds of sugar to twenty quarts of the liquid; pour all into gallon jugs, or casks if you have a large quantity of wine, leave the corks of the jugs or the bung holes open if you use casks, until all the sediment has risen to the top; then draw it off in bottles. It is best to add one gill of the best brandy to each gallon of the wine when putting it into bottles; it improves by age. When sweeter wine is preferred, put one pound of sugar to each quart of the liquid.

Raspberry and gooseberry wine is made the same way, but with less sugar.

A GOOD WAY TO MAKE PUNCH.—Take two large fresh lemons, with rough skins, and some lumps of the best white sugar. Rub the sugar over the lemons till it has absorbed all the yellow part of the skin; then put into the bowl these lumps and as much more as the juice of the lemons may require, according to taste; then squeeze the lemon juice upon the sugar; press the juice and sugar well together. Then mix this up well with boiling water till the water is rather cool. When this mixture is to your taste, take brandy and rum, in equal quantities, and add them to it. Mix the whole together again; the quantity of liquor must be according to your taste. Two good lemons are generally enough to make four quarts of punch, including a quart of liquor, with half a pound of sugar; but this will depend on the taste, and on the strength of the spirit. The sherbet may be strained before the liquor is put in; some strain the lemon juice before it is put to the sugar, which is not proper, as when the pulp and sugar are well mixed it adds to the richness of the punch.

MILK PUNCH—Pare six oranges and six lemons as thin as you can, grate them afterwards with sugar to get the flavor; steep the peels in a bottle of rum or brandy for two days; squeeze the lemons and oranges on two pounds of sugar, add to it four quarts of water and one quart of new milk, boiling hot; stir the rum or brandy into the above and run it through a jelly bag until perfectly clear. Bottle and cork close im-immediately.

GINGER BEER.—Three gallons of cold water, one quart of molasses, one tablespoonful of cream of tartar, three tablespoonfuls of ground ginger, and one quart of yeast; mix all together in a large vessel and let it stand for six hours, it may then be bottled and fit for drinking as early as possible.

RASPBERRY VINEGAR.—Put a pound of fine fruit into a china bowl, and pour upon it a quart of the best white wine vinegar; next day strain the liquor on a pound of fresh raspberries, and the following day do the same; but do not squeeze the fruit, only drain the liquor as dry as you can from it; the last time pass it through a canvass, previously wet with vinegar, to prevent waste; put it into a stone jar, with a pound of sugar to every pint of juice; stir it when melted, then put the jar into a saucepan of water on the stove; let it simmer, and skim it. When cold, bottle it. This is one of the most useful preparations that can be kept in a house for complaints of the chest, and pleasant as a drink. Do not use glazed nor metal vessels for it. Dose: one or two large spoonfuls in a tumbler of water.

RHUBARB VINEGAR.—Take a dozen good sized stalks of rhubarb, mash them in a tub, and then pour on five gallons of water; let it stand twenty-four hours; then strain and add nine pounds of brown sugar, and a little brewers' yeast; let it remain in a warm place about a month, when it must be strained and put back in the cask again, until it becomes vinegar.

Pickles, Vegetables, Etc.

Observations on Pickles

Keep them closely covered, and have a perforated wooden spoon tied to each jar, all metal being injurious; they should be well secured from the air. Large jars should seldom be opened. Small ones for the different pickles in use should be kept for common supply, into which all that are not eaten may be returned, and the tops closely covered.

Acids dissolve the lead that is in the tinning of saucepans. When it is necessary to boil vinegar, put it in a stone jar on the stove. Pickles should never be put into glazed jars, as salt and vinegar penetrate the glaze, which is poisonous. Prepare vegetables for pickling in the following manner: Cauliflower should be cut in branches; young French beans whole; cucumbers, choose the least seedy sort, cut them in slices or quarters if not too large; all must be salted, drained and dried in the sun, then pour over them boiling vinegar, and in twelve hours drain; no salt must be used. Put the spice, garlic, a quarter of a pound of mustard seed, and as much vinegar as you think enough for the quantity you are to pickle into a large stone jar, and one ounce of turmeric, to be ready by the time the vegetables shall be dried; when they are ready observe the following directions: put some of them into a stone jar, and pour over one quart of boiling vinegar; next day take out the vegetables, and when drained put them into a large stock jar, and pour the boiling vinegar over the vegetables; let them stand a night; to every gallon of vinegar put two ounces of ground mustard, mixing by degrees with a little of the vinegar boiling hot; the vinegar must be scalded first and left to get cold, before adding the spice; let the jar be tight. This pickle will not be ready for a year; but a small jar can be made in a fortnight in this way: scald the cauliflower in water, after salting and drying as above, but without the preparative vinegar, then pour the vinegar that has the spice and garlic in it boiling hot over it. If at any time the vegetables have swelled properly, boiling the pickle and pouring it over them hot will plump them.

TO PICKLE WALNUTS.—Let them be gathered fresh, before the kernel is formed in them, and soak them for nine days in strong salt and water; take them out and put them in the sun for three days, after which take some vinegar that has been boiled with whole ginger, whole allspice and whole peppers; let the vinegar be poured over them warm; they will be ready in four months.

TO PICKLE NASTURTIUMS.—Let them be in salt water three days, with a little alum; then take them out of the water and pour boiling vinegar over them, with whole allspice, ginger and pepper; let them be put in bottles; they can be mixed with other pickles.

TO PICKLE PEACHES.—Take a quarter of a pound of sugar to one pint of vinegar and scald the peaches, they should not be quite ripe; put them with some mace, allspice, cloves and nutmeg; when boiled take out the spice, and put the peaches in a jar; observe that the vinegar covers them, and put them away in a dry cool place. Pears and plums can be pickled the same way.

DUTCH CUCUMBERS.—Choose them rather small, but they must be very fresh and firm; let them be well washed and placed in a barrel that will hold water; cover them with water that has been boiled with salt, and been well skimmed and left to cool; then pour the water over the cucumbers, with some red peppers, grape vine leaves and dill seed, between each layer; be careful not to put too much salt in, as the longer they stand the more will the salt penetrate through; it is the best way to boil the pickle, as it will keep much longer; they can be ready for use in three weeks; they must be well covered, not too heavy pressed, as it is apt to mash the pickles.

RED CABBAGE.—Choose fine firm cabbages, trim off the outside leaves, quarter the cabbage, take out the large stalks, slice the quarters into a pan, and sprinkle salt between each layers, not too much, or it will spoil the color; let it remain till next day, then shake it well, that the brine may run off; put it in jars, cover with good vinegar, black pepper and allspice, of each an ounce, pounded ginger, half an ounce of salt to every quart of vinegar, and some cayenne pepper.

ONIONS.—The best for pickling are the small, silver skinned; make a brine and put them into it hot; let them remain one or two days, and drain them quite dry; put them into clean jars, and cover them with hot pickle. To every quart of onions put one ounce of sliced horseradish, black pepper, allspice, salt, with or without mustard seed. Cover them well with the pickle or they will not keep good.

TO PICKLE LEMONS.—Make a brine sufficiently strong to float an egg on top; then choose some lemons with smooth skins, perforate them with a silver fork, and put them in the brine; cover close; if the sun is hot let them remain for a week, or put them on the range for a week, but do not allow them to boil.

MUSTARD PICKLE.—Take a quarter of a pound of turmeric, one ounce of mace, one of cloves, one pound of English mustard, two gallons of the best vinegar, and one pint of mustard seed; mix all smoothly together, and let it come to a boil. When it is cold, put it in a jar and keep it stirred; put some cabbage in salt water for three days, then lay it in the sun for three days, turn it often, and pour boiling water over it; then wring it out in a clean towel, and it is ready for the above pickle. The spires should be ground and put in a bag.

SWEET PICKLE.—To six pounds of brown sugar put two gallons of the best vinegar, and spice to taste; boil all together for ten minutes, then set it to cool; fill the jars with the vegetables or fruits to be pickled and pour over the vinegar. When cool, if there should be a white scum on the top, boil the vinegar again, and add a little more sugar. When cold add it to the jar again. Peaches or any kind of fruit are nice pickled in this way.

TOMATO SAUCE.—Take a gallon of tomatoes, a quart of apple vinegar, two tablespoonfuls of ground black pepper, two of salt, two of English mustard, a spoonful of spices, onion, if preferred, or garlic, one teaspoonful of cayenne pepper; boil slowly for six hours, stir it frequently, then skim it and bottle. Boil it in a porcelain stewpan, as copper or brass stewpans would be dangerous.

PEPPER KETCHUP.—Take two quarts of red or green pepper pods, and split them; boil in enough water to cover them; stir and break them while boiling; strain them through a colander first, then through a sieve. To two quarts of the pulp add one quart of vinegar, two or three spears of garlic, if liked, an onion minced fine, a tablespoonful of salt, one of cloves, and one of allspice. Boil for two hours; if it is too thick put in more vinegar. If you use red pods it makes a fine red ketchup.

CUCUMBER KETCHUP.—Grate three dozen large cucumbers and twelve white onions, put three handfuls of salt over them; they must be prepared the day before, and in the morning lay them to drain; soak a cupful and a half of mustard seed, then drain them and add to the cucumbers two spoonfuls of whole pepper; put them in a jar, cover with vinegar, and cork tight. Keep in a dry place.

CHOW.—Grate two sticks of horseradish, and add a spoonful of turmeric, two tablespoonfuls of celery seed, four tablespoonfuls of sugar, and three tablespoonfuls of mustard seed; cover it with sufficient vinegar; pack it in wide mouthed bottles, and cork it tight. November is the proper month to make it.

TO STEW MUSHROOMS.—You must be careful to become acquainted with the different sorts of things called by this name, as the death of many people has been caused by inexperienced persons carelessly using the poisonous kinds. The eatable mushrooms first appear very small, and of a round form, on a little stock; they grow very fast, and the upper part and stalk are white, as the size increases the under part gradually opens, and shows a fungy fur of a very fine salmon color, which continues more or less till the mushroom has gained some size, and then turns to a dark brown.

These marks should be attended to, and likewise if the skin can be easily parted from the edges and middle. Those that have a white or yellow fur should be avoided, though many of them have the same smell, but not so strong, as the proper sort.

The large buttons are best, and the small tops while the fur is still red. Rub them with salt and a bit of flannel; cut out the fur and take off the skin from the others, sprinkle them with salt, and put into a stewpan with some pepper corns; simmer slowly till done; then put a small bit of butter, some flour, and two spoonfuls of cream. Give them one boil, and serve with sippets of bread.

KALE.—Cut out the stalks, and put the leaves to boil in boiling water and salt; when they are nearly done, pour off the water and cover with fresh; when soft enough, take them up and put them in a saucepan with a little butter and browned flour; stir it quickly and serve hot.

CABBAGE.—Wash it well under the hydrant; be particular there are no worms hidden under the leaves; let the water be boiling, put the cabbage in, and let it boil for three-quarters of an hour, with a good handful of salt. When you wash it, put a good lump of salt in the water, it will clear the worms off; dish it up with a strainer; let the water be drained off; cut the cabbage across several times with a knife. If boiled with meat it needs no other gravy, but if boiled by itself a sauce can be made to throw over it. The English people eat it as it is taken out of the water.

TO COOK SPINACH.—Wash it well after it is picked, in a number of waters till clean; it is always best to let the hydrant run over it, as that clears off the sand better; when well cleaned put it in a saucepan with some salt, without water, and cook it till tender, without the cover being on the boiler; for all vegetables, except potatoes, to reish the spinach this way: fry some onions in fat, and chop up the spinach with a handful of flour; then add the onions seasoned with some salt, cayenne pepper and a little nutmeg; return the spinach to the saucepan, and add some good gravy to it; let it cook for half an hour, and dish up with poached eggs.

TO COOK POTATOES.—When nicely peeled and the eyes taken out, put them in a saucepan with water, not quite covered and a handful of salt; let them boil for half an hour; when done strain them, and let them stand over the fire for a couple of minutes, and then put a nice clean cloth over them till ready to dish up. Potatoes should not stand long before being served, as they lose their flavor.

The way to boil all green vegetables: Put them in boiling water, and skim them well, add some salt and a small pieces of soda; be sure not to cover them, as that will preserve the color better, keep them well under the water; half an hour generally suffices.

TO BOIL CORN.—Take some full grown young and tender corn, strip the husks and silk off the ears, leaving one husk on, as it adds to the sweetness and keeps it hot; boil fast for half an hour, until tender, then send hot to the table; to be eaten with butter, if for breakfast.

HOW TO MAKE SUCCOTASH, IN WINTER.—Take some small white beans, soak them over night, and then put them on to boil; when they are half done add the corn, and let them boil till quite tender, then add butter, salt, and pepper.

OYSTER PLANT, OR SALSIFY.—Scrape the root the same as parsnips; boil them till tender, then mash them; add an egg and some powdered crackers. Make them into cakes, and fry them in butter or fat. Send to table while hot.

CABBAGE, (*Red or white.*)—Take a good piece of brisket, and boil till tender; one hour and a half before it is finished have some nice hard cabbage cut up thin; put it to the stew with some salt, pepper, and whole allspice, with half a pint of vinegar; thicken with a tablespoonful of flour; a little sugar may be added.

Sour krout may be prepared as above, but there need be no vinegar added, unless preferred.

TO STEW ONIONS.—Peel some onions, fry gently of a fine brown, then put them in a stewpan, with some butter, a little water, pepper, and salt; when done, thicken with a little flour; stew for two hours.

TOMATO SAUCE.—Scald and peel them, and put a little water in the saucepan, with a piece of butter, some pepper and salt; stew them well; the more they are stewed the better. Serve cold.

EGG PLANT.—Cut it into slices, about a quarter of an inch thick, and let them soak in cold water and salt for two or three hours, then fry them with egg and flour a nice brown color.

MACARONI, FRIED WITH ONIONS.—Take six eggs, and as much flour as will roll out thin as frimsels, and let them dry, cut as for luxion; boil in boiling water, and then pour them in cold water; fry some onions a nice brown, and make the macaroni hot again; throw the hot onions over the macaroni and serve.

TO BOIL ASPARAGUS.—Have ready a pot of boiling water, with a good handful of salt; boil for twenty minutes, not longer, (as it spoils the flavor;) have ready some nice butter sauce, and place the asparagus on some nice buttered toast in the dish.

Cauliflowers and peas may be cooked in the same manner. Peas may have some fresh mint added.

PEAS.—Young peas require only fifteen minutes to boil; if older a very small bit of carbonate of soda thrown into the water softens them. Season with butter, pepper, salt, and mint, according to taste.

STRINGED BEANS.—If young they will only require fifteen minutes' boiling, but if old half an hour. Season well with either gravy or butter, pepper and salt.

Lima beans may be cooked the same way.

ONIONS.—Boil them in water first, when they are nearly cooked pour off the water and add milk; boil them till done; take them up and serve quite hot, with butter, pepper, and salt.

SQUASHES.—These should be boiled whole, or cut in halves, and mashed without peeling, as the skin is the sweetest part; but if the skin is thick and tough, peel and mash them. Season with pepper, salt and butter.

ARTICHOKES.—The portion eaten is the under side of the artichoke before the flower opens, the head is removed and boiled. It is eaten with a butter sauce.

CAULIFLOWER.—Wrap it up in a cloth, and put it into a saucepan of boiling water; let it parboil, then put it in cold water, until very near the time it is wanted, then boil it for ten minutes, it makes it firmer than when boiled for half an hour. Serve with a sauce.

Broccoli is cooked the same way.

FRITTERS.—Make them the same as for pancakes by dropping a small quantity in the pan, or make them plainer, and put pared apple, sliced and cored, into the batter, and fry some of it with each slice; currants or lemons sliced as thin as paper make an agreeable change. Fritters should be served in a folded napkin, in the dish. Rice can be made the same way, but first boil to a jelly, and then leave to cool.

POTATO FRITTERS.—Boil two large potatoes, grate them very fine, beat four yolks and three whites of eggs, add to the above one large spoonful of cream, another of sweet wine, a squeeze of lemon, a little nutmeg, beat all for at least half an hour, it will be very light; put a great deal of either oil or butter in the pan, and drop a spoonful of the batter at a time in the pan; fry them and serve. To be eaten with the following sauce: a glass of white wine, the juice of a lemon, a little essence of almonds and some white sugar, warmed together.

APPLE CHARLOTTE.—Cut as many very thin slices of bread as will cover the bottom and line the sides of a baking dish, but rub it thick with butter. Put apples, cut in thin slices, into the dish in layers till full, strewing sugar and bits of butter between; soak as many slices of bread in warm milk as will cover the whole; over which lay a plate and weight, to keep the bread on the apples. Bake slowly for three hours. To a middling sized dish use half a pound of butter for the whole.

BATTER WITH MEAT.—Make the batter with water instead of milk; pour a little into the bottom of the dish; then season a nice shoulder of mutton, put it into the dish, and pour the remainder of the batter over it; bake in a slow oven.

MEAT STEWED WITH CARROTS.—Take a piece of brisket, about four or five pounds, and put it into a stewpan with a quart and a pint of cold water, and six large onions; after it has been skimmed, add a peck of carrots, that have been well scraped, washed and cut into strips, with pepper, salt, and a little nutmeg; let them stew for several hours till tender; when it is nearly done thicken with a tablespoonful of flour and a tablespoonful of coarse brown sugar.

KERTOFFLE CHARLOTTE.—Take a dozen raw potatoes and scrape them on a grater; take some bread crumbs, about a pound, and two eggs well beaten; season with pepper, salt, ginger, nutmeg, a quarter of a pound of fat, and bake in the oven a nice brown.

BUBBLE AND SQUEAK.—Strew some pepper on some slices of cold meat; fry them in some drippings of roast meat, with some cold cabbage, chopped small. Then take the beef out of the frying pan, and lay the cabbage in it; sprinkle some pepper and salt over it. Move the pan all the time over the fire. Lay the cabbage in the middle of the dish, and the beef around it.

CELERY STEW.—Take a piece of brisket, about three pounds, and stew it in a pint of water, with some onions, and four or five celery roots, cut up small, add some bread crumbs; thicken with a tablespoonful of flour, some pepper and salt.

ALL VEGETABLES may be stewed with sugar. They must be chopped very fine, and seasoned with some good gravy or fat, pepper, salt, etc., and thickened with a small quantity of flour. Germans prefer them cooked in this way; but the English eat them cooked in water.

TO BOIL POTATOES IN THE SKIN.—Take some good sized ones, wash them well, cut a piece off the top, and take out the eyes; set them on in cold water, with a handful of salt; boil gently for half an hour; strain off good and dry; peel for the table.

MUSTARD FOR THE CASTORS.—Take a tablespoonful of mustard, mix it smooth with a tablespoonful of salt, half a teaspoonful of sifted sugar, if liked, six tablespoonfuls of water or vinegar; horseradish is good with it. Do not make more than will last for two days.

TO ROAST COFFEE.—Use either a patent roaster or the Irish mop roaster; to every three pounds of coffee add a little sweet oil, and two teaspoonfuls of pounded sugar; then roast the berries; it makes the flavor of the coffee richer; it is preferable to chicory, although some persons prefer chicory; the quantity is a quarter of a pound of chicory to a pound of coffee.

HOW TO MAKE GOOD COFFEE.—Put four tablespoonfuls of fresh ground coffee in a coffeepot with a strainer, and pour over it four breakfast cupfuls of boiling water, and two cupfuls of boiling milk; boil up for two or three minutes, add a couple of egg-shells and half a cupful of cold water; let it settle, and stand by the fire to keep hot for ten minutes.

MISCELLANEOUS.

TO CLEAN PAINT.—Never use a cloth, but take off the dust with a long-haired hand brush. With care, paint will look well for a length of time; when soiled, dip a sponge or a bit of flannel into soda water, wash it quickly, and dry immediately, or the strength of the soda will eat off the color. When wainscot requires scouring it should be done from the top downward, and the soda be prevented from running on the unclean part as much as possible, or marks will be made which will appear after the whole is finished. One person should dry with old linen as fast as the other has scoured the dirt and washed the soda off.

TO CLEAN PAPER HANGINGS.—First brush off the dust, then divide a white loaf of bread, eight days old, into eight parts. Take the crust into your hand, and, beginning at the top of the paper, wipe it downwards in the lightest manner with the crumb. Do not rub cross or go upwards. The dust off the paper and the crumbs will fall together. Observe you must not wipe above half a yard at a time, and after doing all the upper parts go round again, beginning a little above where you left off. If you do not rub it very lightly, you will make the dirt adhere to the paper. It will look like new paper if properly done.

LAVENDER WATER.—To one pint of rectified spirits of wine add essential oil of lavender, one ounce; essence of ambergris, two drachms. Put all in a quart bottle, and shake it well.

FLOOR CLOTHS.—Those should be chosen that are painted on a fine cloth that is well covered with the color, and the flowers on which do not rise much above the ground, as they wear out first. The durability of the cloth will depend much on these two particulars, but more especially on the time it has been painted and the quality of the colors. If they have not been allowed sufficient time for becoming thoroughly dry, a very little use will injure them; and as they are very expensive articles, care in preserving them is necessary.

It is best to keep them yourself some time before using them; hang them up where they will receive the air, or lay them down in a spare room where they cannot be trodden on.

TO CLEAN FLOOR CLOTH.—Sweep it, then wipe it with a flannel cloth, and where dust and spots are to be moved, rub with a waxed flannel cloth, and then with a dry one, use but little wax; rub only enough with the latter to give a little smoothness, or it may endanger falling. Washing now and then with milk, after the above sweeping and drying, and rubbing it, gives a beautiful appearance, and it is less slippery in walking over.

TO CLEAN CARPETS.—Take up the carpets and let them be well beaten; then lay them down and brush both sides with a hand brush; turn the right side upwards, and scour with ox gall, soap, and clean water dry them with a linen cloth; then lay them on the grass, or hang them up to dry. When sweeping or dusting carpets always cover everything up, until the dust settles. When matting is washed, use salt in the water.

HOW TO SCRUB BOARDS TO LOOK WHITE.—After washing them very nicely, clean with soap and warm water and a brush; wash them with a large flannel and clean water; put a handful of soda in the water; do not leave a spot untouched, and clean straight up and down, not crossing from board to board; then dry, with a clean, coarse cloth, rubbing hard up and down in the same way. The floors should not be often wetted, but very thoroughly when done, and once a week dry rubbed with hot sand and a hard brush, the lengthway of the boards.

TO TAKE STAINS OUT OF MARBLE, No. 1.—Mix unslacked lime, in fine powder, with the strongest soap lye, and apply instantly with a painter's brush, cover the marble with the mixture. In two months' time wash it off perfectly clean, then have ready a fine thick lather of soap boiled in soft water, dip a brush in it, and scour the marble with powder, not as common cleaning. This will, by very good rubbing, give a beautiful polish. Wash off the soap and finish with a smooth, hard brush till the end be effected.

TO TAKE STAINS OUT OF MARBLE, No. 2.—An equal quantity of fresh spirits of vitriol and lemon juice being mixed in a bottle, shake it well, wet the spots, and in a few minutes rub with soft linen till they disappear.

TO CEMENT BROKEN CHINA.—Beat some lime into powder; sift it through a fine muslin cloth, then tie some in a thin muslin cloth; put on the edges of the broken china some white of egg, then dust some lime quickly on the same and unite them exactly.

TO CLEAN TIN COVERS, ETC.—Get the finest whiting; (this is only sold in large cakes, the smaller cakes being mixed with sand;) mix a little of it, powdered, with the least drop of sweet oil, rub well and wipe clean; then dust some dry whiting in a muslin bag over it, and rub bright with a dry leather. The last is to prevent rust, which must be guarded against by wiping dry and putting by the fire, when they come from the table, for, if but once hung up without having the steam wiped out entirely, they will rust outside.

FURNITURE POLISH.—Take one pint of linseed oil, and two wineglassfuls of alcohol, and a wineglassful of vinegar; mix well together; rub the furniture with a linen rag, then rub it dry with a soft cloth, and polish with an old silk handkerchief; wash it occasionally with soap suds, wipe it dry and rub it over with a flannel cloth dipped in linseed oil; wipe all polished furniture with old silk.

HOW TO CLEAN SILKS AND RIBBONS.—Take equal quantities of soft soap, alcohol, and molasses; mix well; then lay the silk on a table and rub the mixture over with a piece of flannel; rinse in cold water, and hang it up to dry. Iron on the wrong side before it gets dry. Deer's horn, sawed up in small pieces and boiled several hours in water, and then strained, is nice to dress silk with; it gives it a stiffness and lustre almost like new. Camphene will extract grease, but it will change the color.

TO TAKE STAINS FROM SILK.—Salt of ammonia mixed with lime will take out stains of wine from silk. It is also good to renew the color, if there are any spots.

TO REMOVE STAINS OF WINE FRUIT, (*after they have been long in the linen.*)—Rub the part on each side with yellow soap; then lay on a mixture of starch in cold water, very thick, rub it well in, and expose the linen to the sun and air, till the stain comes out. If not removed in three or four days, rub that off and renew the process; when dry it may be sprinkled with a little water. Many other stains may be taken out, by dipping the linen in sour buttermilk, and drying in the hot sun; then wash it in cold water, and dry it two or three times a day.

TO TAKE STAINS OUT OF LINEN, No. 1.—Sprinkle some salt on the stains, then take a juicy lemon and rub the linen thoroughly; then dip it in boiling water, and lay in the sun; then apply it again until the stains are removed; with patience you will succeed.

TO TAKE STAINS OUT OF LINEN, No. 2.—Wet the part and lay on it some salt of wormwood; then rub it without diluting it with more water, or let the cloth imbibe a little water without dipping, and hold the part over a lighted match, at a due distance, the spots will be removed by the sulphurous gas.

TO EXTRACT GREASE FROM MERINOS, SILKS, ETC. —Spread on magnesia or powdered French chalk, place on it a piece of brown paper, and let it remain a few hours; then blow it off and put on more; continue this until the grease is removed.

TO TAKE OUT MILDEW.—Mix soft soap with powdered starch, half as much salt, and the juice of a lemon; lay it on both sides of the stain with a painter's brush; let it lie on the grass, day and night, till the stain is out.

TO REMOVE STAINS FROM SILVER.—Soak the silver in lye for three or four hours, then cover it thick with whiting, wet with vinegar; let it dry on, then rub it with dry whiting, and polish it with dry wheat bran. Silver should always be washed in hot water with silver soap, wiped dry, and rubbed with a soft leather, then it will not require so much cleaning.

TO WASH A BLACK LACE VEIL.—Mix beef's gall with water hot enough to bear your hands in; do not rub the veil, but squeeze it through, then rinse in two or three cold waters; in the last put a little indigo, and dry it; scald a small piece of glue, put the veil in to stiffen it; squeeze it out and clap it; lay it on a linen cloth, and make it perfectly smooth, then iron it on the wrong side.

TO REVIVE THE COLOR OF BLACK SILK.—Boil some logwood in water half an hour, then simmer the silk half an hour, take it out and put into the dye a little blue vitriol, or green copperas; cool it and simmer the silk again for half an hour.

TO PRESERVE GILDING AND CLEAN IT.—It is not possible to prevent flies from staining the gilding without covering it; before which blow off the light dust, and pass a feather or clean brush over it; then with strips of paper cover the frames of the glasses, and do not remove it till the flies are all gone. Linen takes off the gilding, and deadens its brightness; it should, therefore, never be used for wiping it. Some means should be used to destroy the flies, as they injure furniture of every kind, and the paper likewise. Bottles hung about with sugar and vinegar, or beer, or flypaper in a plate, just wetted, will attract them; they should be put out of the reach of children.

TO CLEAN PLATE.—Boil an ounce of prepared hartshorn in a quart of water. While on the fire, put into it as much plate as the vessel will hold; let it boil a little, then take it out, drain it over the saucepan, and dry it before the fire. Put in more and serve the same way until you have done. Then put into the water some clean rags, till all is soaked up. When dry, they will do to clean the plate, and are the very best things to clean brass locks and finger-plates on the door. When the plate is quite dry, it must be rubbed bright with leather.

HOW TO MAKE GUM ARABIC STARCH.—Take two ounces of white gum arabic powder, pour on it a pint or more of boiling water as you wish, and some salt, and then having covered it, let it set all night. In the morning, pour it carefully from the dregs into a clean bottle, cork it and keep it for use.

A tablespoonful of gum water stirred into a pint of starch that has been made in this way, will give lawns, either white or black, or printed, a look of newness. It is good when diluted for thin white muslin.

HOW TO GIVE A GLOSS TO SHIRT BOSOMS.—Take half an ounce of white wax, half an ounce of gum arabic, half an ounce of isinglass, a few drops of alcohol, and half a pint of water; mix it well and keep it in a bottle. To a good sized pan of starch, put a teaspoonful of this mixture. Starch the shirt while it is wet; if dry, dip it in hot water, and wring it dry; then starch, rub it in well, spread out the bosom, wipe it over with a clean cloth, then roll it, let it lay for an hour or so and iron. Rice water and isinglass will stiffen thin muslins better than starch.

SEALING FRUIT CANS.—How to know that the fruit can is properly sealed, with canned fruit, and the contents will keep. As soon as it cools, the fruit will slightly shrink, leaving a vacuum at the top, and the bottom of the can will become hollow from the pressure of the external air. This shows that the sealing is complete. Set the can in a warm place, for four or five days; if the hollow remain on the top and bottom then it is all right.

TO CLEAN AN OLD SILK DRESS.—Unpick the dress, and brush it with a velvet brush; then grate two large potatoes into a quart of water; let it stand to settle; then strain quite clear, and sponge the dress with it. Iron the dress on the wrong side, as the ironed side will be shiny.

TO PRESERVE BLANKETS.—The best means to preserve blankets from moths is to fold and lay them on a shelf, well covered with sheets of newspapers, shaking them occasionally. When soiled, they should be washed, not scoured.

HOW TO MAKE POMATUM.—Take a pound of beef marrow, and boil it; then take a pound of lard and mix with the marrow when boiled, and add to it any scent that is preferred; beat together until it is well mixed with a quarter of a pint of castor oil, and bottle off.

BANDOLINE FOR THE HAIR.—Take one ounce and a half of isinglass and two-thirds of a pint of water; pour the water over the isinglass, and let it remain all night. Next day put it to warm till dissolved, then add two wineglasses of spirits of wine. Scent with any oil you prefer, but mix it with the spirits before adding.

TO KEEP THE COLOR OF FLANNELS.—Put them into a pail, and pour boiling water over them; let them lie till cold the first time of washing.

HOW TO MAKE SHOE BLACKING.—Take one pound of well pulverized ivory black, half a pound of loaf sugar, half an ounce of oil of vitriol, six ounces of sweet oil, and one gallon of vinegar; stir it well and it will produce a beautiful polish.

HOW TO CLEAN MUSTY BARRELS.—Put a peck of charcoal in a large barrel, with half a pint of saleratus; pour in boiling water until the barrel is full; cover it up close, and let it remain until it is cold.

TO KEEP AWAY HOUSE VERMIN.—To keep away mosquitoes, attach a piece of flannel, wetted with camphorated spirits and alum, on the top of the bedstead.

Put spearmint around places that are infested with mice; they have a great aversion to it.

TO GET RID OF ANTS.—Wash the shelves with salt and water, and sprinkle salt wherever they may be seen. Set the legs of the safe in tin cups filled with salt water.

TO DESTROY ROACHES.—Sprinkle Scotch snuff in the holes where they come out.

A GOOD BUG POISON.—Take proof spirits, one pint; camphor, two ounces; oil of turpentine, four ounces; corrosive sublimate, one ounce. Mix them all together, and apply with a feather. Keep it out of the way of children, and label it in plain letters, as it is a deadly poison.

SEASONABLE FOOD.

For each month of the year.

JANUARY.

MEATS.—Beef, mutton, veal, house lamb.

POULTRY.—Pheasants, partridges, turkies, pullets, capons, fowls and pigeons.

FISH.—Cod, haddock, rock, perch, whiting, smelts, turbot, plaice, flounders, perch, tench and carp.

VEGETABLES.—Cabbage and sprouts, sorrel, endive, spinach, beet-root, celery, potatoes, parsnips, turnips, broccoli, shalots, lettuce, cress, salsify, cucumbers and asparagus. Mushrooms all the year.

FEBRUARY.

MEATS.—Beef, mutton, veal, house lamb.

POULTRY.—Chickens and ducklings.

FISH.—Cod, haddock, rock, perch, whiting, smelts, turbot, plaice, flounders, perch, tench and carp.

VEGETABLES.—Cabbage and sprouts, sorrel, endive, spinach, beet-root, celery, potatoes, parsnips, turnips, broccoli, shalots, lettuce, cress, salsify, cucumbers, asparagus and kidney beans.

FRUITS.—Pears, apples, nuts, grapes, forced strawberries, medlers and walnuts.

MARCH.

MEATS.—Beef, mutton, veal, house lamb.

POULTRY.—Chickens and ducklings.

FISH.—Cod, haddock, rock, perch, whiting, smelts, turbot, plaice, flounders, perch, tench and carp.

VEGETABLES.—Cabbage and sprouts, sorrel, endive, spinach, beet-root, celery, potatoes, parsnips, turnips, broccoli, shalots, lettuce, cress, salsify, cucumbers, asparagus and kidney beans.

FRUITS.—Pears, apples, nuts, grapes, forced strawberries, medlers and walnuts.

APRIL.

MEATS.—Beef, mutton, veal, lamb.

POULTRY.—Pullets, fowls, chickens, ducklings and pigeons.

FISH.—Shad, rock, perch, smelts, white fish, carp, soles, tench, trout, turbot, salmon, herring, mackerel and halibut. White fish all the year.

VEGETABLES.—Cabbage and sprouts, sorrel, endive, spinach, beet-root, celery, potatoes, parsnips, turnips, broccoli, shalots, lettuce, cress, salsify, cucumbers, asparagus and kidney beans.

MAY.

MEATS.—Beef, mutton, veal, lamb.

POULTRY.—Pullets, fowls, chickens, ducklings and pigeons.

FISH.—Shad, rock, perch, smelts, white fish, carp, soles, tench, trout, turbot, salmon, herring, mackerel and halibut.

VEGETABLES.—Cabbage and sprouts, sorrel, endive, spinach, beet-root celery, parsnips, broccoli, shalots, lettuce, cress, salsify, cucumbers, early potatoes, peas, radishes, French beans, carrots, turnips, cauliflowers, asparagus, artichokes and all kinds of salad from hot house.

JUNE.

MEATS.—Beef, mutton, veal, lamb.

POULTRY.—Pullets, fowls, chickens, ducklings and pigeons.

FISH.—Shad, rock, perch, Spanish mackerel, smelts, white fish, carp, soles, tench, trout, turbot, salmon, herring, mackerel and halibut.

VEGETABLES.—Cabbage and sprouts, sorrel, endive, spinach, beet-root, celery, parsnips, broccoli, shalots, lettuce, cress, salsify, cucumbers, early potatoes, peas, radishes, French beans, carrots, turnips, cauliflower, asparagus, artichokes and all kinds of salad from hot house.

FRUITS.—Strawberries, cherries, melons, green apricots, currants, and green gooseberries, fit for tarts only.

JULY.

MEATS.—Beef, mutton, veal, lamb.

POULTRY.—Pullets, fowls, chickens, pigeons and green geese.

FISH.—Cod, haddock, rock, perch, Spanish mackerel, flounders, mullet, pike, carp and mackerel.

VEGETABLES.—Cabbage and sprouts, sorrel, endive, spinach, beet-root, celery, parsnips, broccoli, shalots, lettuce, cress, salsify, cucumbers, early potatoes, peas, radishes, French beans, carrots, turnips, cauliflower, asparagus, artichokes and all kinds of salad from hot house.

FRUITS.—Strawberries, gooseberries, pine apples, plums of all kinds, cherries, apricots, raspberries, melons, damsons, white, black and red currants, pears, apples, nectarines, grapes, and peaches.

AUGUST.

MEATS.—Beef, mutton, veal, lamb.

POULTRY.—Pullets, fowls, chickens, pigeons and green geese.

FISH.—Cod, haddock, rock, perch, Spanish mackerel, flounders, mullet, pike, carp and mackerel.

VEGETABLES.—Cabbage and sprouts, sorrel, endive, spinach, beet-root, celery, parsnips, broccoli, shalots, lettuce, cress, salsify, cucumbers, early potatoes, peas, radishes, French beans, carrots, turnips, cauliflower, asparagus, artichokes and all kinds of salad from hot house.

FRUITS.—Peaches, plums, filberts, figs, mulberries, cherries, apples, pears nectarines, grapes, pine apples, melons and strawberries.

SEPTEMBER.

MEATS.—Beef, mutton, veal, lamb.

POULTRY.—Pullets, fowls, chickens, pigeons, green geese, turkies and geese.

FISH.—Cod, haddock, rock, perch, Spanish mackerel, flounders, mullet, pike, carp and mackerel.

VEGETABLES.—Cabbage and sprouts, sorrel, endive, spinach, beet-root, celery, parsnips, broccoli, shalots, lettuce, cress, salsify, cucumbers, potatoes, peas, radishes, French beans, carrots, turnips, cauliflower, asparagus, artichokes, and all kinds of salad from hot house.

FRUITS.—Peaches, plums, filberts, figs, mulberries, cherries, apples, pears, nectarines, grapes, pine apples, melons and strawberries.

OCTOBER.

MEATS.—Beef, mutton, veal, lamb.

POULTRY.—Pullets, fowls, chickens, pigeons, turkies, geese, pheasants and partridges.

FISH.—Dories, smelts, pike, perch, halibut, carp, salmon, trout and barbel.

VEGETABLES.—Cabbage and sprouts, sorrel, endive, spinach, beet-root, celery, potatoes, parsnips, turnips, broccoli, shalots, lettuce, cress, salsify, cucumbers and asparagus.

FRUIT.—Peaches, pears, bullaces, grapes, apples, medlars, damsons, filberts, walnuts, nuts and quinces.

NOVEMBER.

MEATS.—Beef, mutton, veal, house lamb.

POULTRY.—Pullets, fowls, chickens, pigeons, turkies, geese, pheasants and partridges.

FISH.—Dories, smelts, pike, perch, halibut, hills, carp, salmon, trout and barbel.

VEGETABLES.—Cabbage and sprouts, sorrel, endive, spinach, beet-root, celery, potatoes, parsnips, turnips, broccoli, shalots, lettuce, cress, salsify, cucumbers and asparagus.

FRUITS.—Peaches, pears, bullaces, grapes, apples, medlars, filberts, walnuts, nuts and quinces.

DECEMBER.

MEATS.—Beef, mutton, veal, house lamb.

POULTRY.—Geese, turkies, pullets, pigeons, capons and fowls.

FISH.—Turbot, gurnets, soles, carp and codlings.

VEGETABLES.—Cabbage and sprouts, sorrel, endive, spinach, beet-root, celery, potatoes, parsnips, turnips, broccoli, shalots, lettuce, cress, salsify, cucumbers and asparagus.

HINTS TO HOUSEKEEPERS.

To enable young housekeepers to vary the viands to be placed upon the table, I would recommend the dishes that may be obtained in their different seasons, and give a variety for one week; these can be changed as persons may desire. We will commence with Monday. As that day is set apart for washing, I would advise any easily cooked breakfast and a cold dinner, as servants are much hurried on that day. It may be that there is but one servant, and she, perhaps, not very competent; and then the lady of the house may be too delicate to see to the arrangement of the table, it would be impossible to have a hot dinner properly cooked.

MONDAY, FOR BREAKFAST.—In spring, some good coffee, with hot milk, made in the Mocha coffee pot, which is highly recommended, and can be purchased at Griffith & Page's store, No. 1004 Arch street, Philadelphia; also some good Souchong tea for those who prefer it, nice soft toast, buttered, with boiling milk poured over it. Make the toast as follows: Cut a piece of baker's bread, a day old, one-half an inch thick, toast it a light brown, butter while it is hot and press it with the knife while buttering to make it soft; then pour two tablespoonfuls of boiling milk over it and cover it over with a plate. Serve while hot. Then prepare some boiled eggs, and a dish of thinly smoked salmon. At a side table, prepared separately, there may be some remnants of cold meat or steak for those who do not like fish or who prefer meat to any other relish; in this case cold boiled potatoes can be fried instead of the milk or buttered toast.

MONDAY, FOR DINNER.—If there should be any remnants from the dinner of the day previous, it would serve well for the Monday dinner, and I think it would be the better plan to have larger joints the day previous, so as to supply the Monday dinner; in cold weather it could be nicely warmed over. See directions for warming or hashing cold meats.

First Course for Monday.—Cold salt beef, or roast; potatoes baked in their skin, or boiled potatoes mashed with some prepared gravy or roast meat drippings, pepper and salt; or they can be peeled and baked in plenty of fat, and seasoned with sage and onions. In the spring season, some good salads, as in directions for salad. Horseradish mixed with vinegar. The cloth must never be set without salt and bread on the table for the purpose of a blessing.

For Dessert.—If there should have been some pudding left from the day previous it could be warmed up in this way: Put the pudding in a deep basin, cover it, place it in a pan of water and then put it in the oven; this will prevent it from burning; let it remain in the oven for one hour and a half. Pies, or any fruit that may be in season can be used; remnants of stews and poultry can be called into requisition.

MONDAY, FOR SUPPER.—Bread and butter, tea and coffee and ice water. In the spring and during the summer I would recommend a pretty bouquet of flowers in the middle of the table; their fragrance refreshes the eye and gratifies the mind, as there is so much sweet language embodied in flowers.

To continue our repast. Prepare some scrambled eggs in this way: Put a piece of butter the size of a walnut in a frying pan; break twelve eggs, but do not separate the whites and yolks; season with salt and pepper; stir the eggs from the bottom of the pan until they are cooked. Spread the eggs on some nice soft well buttered toast, and serve while hot. Some sardines or pickled herring cut up thin after being soaked for an hour and skimmed. Some stewed or uncooked fruit.

TUESDAY, FOR BREAKFAST.—Let those whose duty it is to go to market be there early in order to get the best and freshest articles and send them home early to be cooked in good season for breakfast. Tea and coffee and ice water, hot rolls, as in directions for bread and butter, broiled shad, radishes, watercress, eggs and fried potatoes; strawberries are wholesome. Meat, if preferred, prepared as in directions for Monday.

TUESDAY, FOR DINNER.—*First Course.* A fine piece of the first cut of the ribs roasted, about five pounds, and side dish of stews, for a family of eight persons; boiled and baked potatoes, reished spinach or peas, celery and salads.

For Dessert.—Fruit of any kind.

TUESDAY, FOR SUPPER.—Choose a thick cut of halibut, boil as in directions, and serve with a nice butter sauce; radishes, salad, tea and coffee and ice water, bread and butter, and hot biscuit made this way: In one pound of flour mix one teaspoonful of carbonate of soda, twice that quantity of cream of tartar and one ounce of butter with a pint of sweet milk; roll the dough half an inch thick and cut it with a small biscuit cutter; bake in a quick oven. Stewed fruit and cakes.

WEDNESDAY, FOR BREAKFAST.—Griddle cakes as in directions, coffee with hot milk, tea and ice water; cold fried fish in oil, and pickled or Dutch herring. Berries in season.

WEDNESDAY, FOR DINNER.—*First Course.* A nice spring soup, a shoulder of mutton roasted, to be eaten with currant jam, or a leg of mutton boiled and served with caper sauce, an entree of cold meat left from the day previous; vegetables, broccoli sprouts, salads and boiled potatoes, ice water, etc.

For Dessert.—Boiled fruit puddings as in directions.

WEDNESDAY, FOR SUPPER.—German stewed fish, bread and butter, some hot light biscuit, tea, coffee, etc., light sponge cake and fruit.

THURSDAY, FOR BREAKFAST.—Hot biscuit, omelette, and poached eggs prepared in this way: Have in the frying pan some boiling water, with salt; break the eggshell and put the egg in without disturbing the whites and yolks, and as they boil, skim; when the whites are set they are done; put a piece of butter and a little salt on each egg; if they are preferred to be hard let them remain a little longer on the fire. Dish them up on well buttered toast. Coffee with hot and cold milk, tea and ice water. Side table with rare or well done beefsteak; to cook the steak rare, let there be a good clear fire; put the gridiron on the fire and let it get hot; then place a good thick steak on top; do not let it cook too close to the fire; turn it with two forks and double the steak to save the gravy; do not prick the meat but stick the fork into the fat, turn it two or three times; when done, turn it on a dish and sprinkle salt and pepper on it; put a half pint of boiling water on the dish to make the gravy, and season it with salt and pepper. Eat while it is hot with some nice hot boiled potatoes. Horseradish in vinegar and mustard, pickles, watercress, cucumbers or lettuce salad.

THURSDAY, FOR DINNER.—*First Course.* A fillet of roast veal seasoned with veal stuffing as in directions, a side dish of stewed steak with chestnuts. I would not recommend soup every day as it causes flatulency. Vegetables, green peas, stewed turnips and salads; stewed prunes, etc.

For Dessert.—Stewed rhubarb and apple fritters.

THURSDAY, FOR SUPPER.—Bread and butter, tea, coffee with hot milk, and ice water; anchovies washed and parted in two, the bones taken out, and placed tastefully on a dish; watercress, radishes and salads; green peas boiled and served up with a lump of butter in the middle of the dish, seasoned with pepper, salt, and mint, if preferred; boiled potatoes, and chestnut cake made in this way: Boil and mash two pounds of chestnuts and add a quarter of a pound of white sugar, two ounces of butter, the yolks of eight eggs well beaten; beat all the ingredients well together, adding spices according to taste. Line a pie plate with puff paste, put in the mixture and bake a light brown.

FRIDAY, FOR BREAKFAST.—Hot baker's rolls, coffee, etc , bread and butter, codfish balls or some pickled fish, and fruits. Side table with cold meats and salads.

FRIDAY, FOR DINNER.—As this is the day preparatory to the Sabbath it is generally a busy one, so a short dinner will be most convenient. If in spring, the soup will be prepared for the Sabbath. The meat, when nicely boiled, would make a good dinner for this day, with some salads, potatoes boiled and mashed, or sausage (wosht) boiled with rice; when the sausage is done take it out and cut it in slices and cover with eggs fried in fat. Bread and salt, or any easily cooked meats, such as steak, liver or mutton chops.

For Dessert.—A piece of the paste left from dishes prepared for the Sabbath, or raw fruit.

FRIDAY NIGHT OR SABBATH SUPPER.—Coffee with hot milk, tea and ice water; white or brown stewed fish as in directions, cold fish fried in oil, or hot, fried in butter, German puffs, hot or cold, some lady finger cakes, salads, horseradish with the white stewed fish.

For Dessert.—Fruits, or ice cream made in this way: Take one quart of very rich cream, it must be sweet, and beat it quite stiff in a small churn; boil one quart of the morning's milk over a pan of water and thicken it with a tablespoonful of arrowroot, but do not make it too thick; add a quarter of a pound of loaf sugar, the rind of a lemon, or vanilla; strain all this through a sieve, add it to the cream and mix thoroughly: the cream should be made very sweet as it loses much of the flavoring and sweetness in freezing. Take care not to beat the cream too long or it will come to butter.

Ice cream without using cream can be made in this way: Take one quart of new milk; scald one-half of it and thicken with three tablespoonfuls of wheaten flour; boil quickly until the rawness of the flour disappears, and let it become quite smooth, about the consistency of cream; stir it by degrees, while it is hot, into the other half of the cold milk; flavor with any essence, sweeten well and strain all through a sieve. It is best to boil the milk over water to prevent it burning. If made properly it will be taken for good rich cream.

SATURDAY OR SABBATH BREAKFAST.—It is usual on Friday for persons of our faith to use raisin wine to say the blessing of the sanctification. It is placed on the table with the salt and twist. We are not allowed to cook fresh viands on the Sabbath, so we can have the fish that was cooked on Friday, the same as for the Friday supper. Tea, coffee with hot milk, etc., some stewed fruit, small tarts, butter cakes, soda cakes or any of the cakes as in recipes.

SATURDAY, FOR DINNER.—Dishes as prepared for Friday.

First Course.—Frimsel soup, as that will keep best over night; vegetable soup would be likely to spoil. Either a brown stew and balls made of giblets, etc., or white stew and balls.

Second Course.—Cold roast fowl or turkey with salads; potatoes mashed in fat or gravy and made into a pretty shape and baked a light brown; reished spinach warmed over.

For Dessert.—Apple pies, stewed rhubarb or biscuit, nuts, apples, oranges, raisins, almonds and wine.

SATURDAY, FOR SUPPER.—There is not much variety required for this meal. As we cannot cook on this day, the remnants of cold fish or dessert from dinner will serve with tea, coffee, etc.

SUNDAY, FOR BREAKFAST.—Tomato toast, cold dry toast, bread and butter, hot muffins as in directions, tea, coffee, etc., some fried potatoes, and picked codfish prepared in this way: Pick the fish in small pieces, the smaller the better; be sure to have it soaked over night; put the fish in a saucepan with sufficient water to cover it; season with a quarter of a pound of butter and a little pepper; thicken with a teaspoonful of flour and let it boil for twenty minutes; then add two well beaten eggs; be sure not to curdle it. Some persons boil eggs hard, chop them up small and mix them in the gravy. Asparagus with butter sauce.

SUNDAY, FOR DINNER.—This is the day the husbands are at home, then something good must be prepared in honor of the lords of the household. Ladies need not be at a loss to know what to have, when they have examined this book.

First Course.—Mock turtle or any kind of soup as set forth in the recipes. Brown chicken soup made this way: Cut up some veal, beef and chicken, fry them in fat; put them in a saucepan with three quarts of water, and cover close and let it boil slowly; skim it well; season with salt, cayenne pepper, nutmeg, parsley, grated carrots, some turnips cut small, and two onions; take off all the fat; when the soup is well done strain it, and then add the chicken that has been minced; thicken the soup with some brown flour, and let it boil for ten minutes; to prevent its burning put a plate on the bottom of the saucepan. Toast some bread, cut it up in squares, and put it in the tureen with the chicken, minced fine, and serve it up with the soup quite hot. A fine thick piece of halibut, or rock fish, or salmon served with either a lemon or fennel sauce without butter, fat substituted will answer just as well.

Second Course.—Either roast turkey, roast goose, or roast duck, seasoned with sage and onions, as in directions for roast ducks, or roast lamb and mint sauce.

Entrees.—Calf's feet and veal stew, potatoes, mashed and boiled, peas and asparagus, broccoli sprouts, mashed turnips and boiled onions.

Dessert.—Strawberry pudding made this way: Take two quarts of strawberries, half a pound of loaf sugar, two tablespoonfuls of clarified fat and six eggs; beat all well together with two ounces of grated bread crumbs or lady fingers; put some light paste around a pie plate, but not at the bottom, and put in the mixture; when it is all baked have ready some meringue, as in directions, put over the top and bake in a slow oven; it can be eaten either hot or cold. An apple stephon, or boiled rhubarb pudding, as in directions for boiled puddings. Fruits, Oranges, apples, nuts, almonds and raising. A cup of black coffee or tea.

SUNDAY, FOR SUPPER.—Tea, coffee, etc., scraps of cold fried and stewed fish, omelette, Dutch herring with salads; butter cakes, pound cake or matrimony cake; charlotte russe made in this way: Cut out the inside of a sponge cake, leaving the sides whole; have ready some warm blanc-mange and spread on the cake alternately with a layer of marmalade, until the mould is full. The marmalade must be thinner than the blanc-mange, and let the last layer be blanc-mange to make it look smooth. Chocolate pudding and stewed or raw fruits, may be used instead.

CULINARY UTENSILS, ETC.

Articles which should be in all kitchens.

Let every thing be put in its place. King Solomon says: "there is a time for all things." Children cannot be too early taught the importance of regularity and order. Habits of industry may be early formed and prove a blessing in after life; a bad regulated household, where there is no system, frugality, or neatness, is a bad example for children. Never allow your things to lay around, trusting to the domestic to put them in their places; no matter how many servants you keep, it is a bad habit. If the superior sets a bad example, the servant cannot be blamed for following it.

A well furnished range.
Apple corer and peeler.
A rack for the plates to drain in.
A knife and saw together for cutting the bones of the meat and poultry.
A clock to keep good time.
A wire safe, for cold meat and fish.
A butter print.
A market basket.
Baking pans.
Bread cloths, to put round the dough when set to rise in the winter.
Bread grater.
Bread jars, with covers to keep out vermin.
Bread toaster.
Biscuit cutter.
Biscuit board.
Basting ladle.
Brooms.
Brushes.
Bottle cleaner.
Butter cooler.
Butter bowl.
Bags for different sweet dried herbs.
Brushes.
Cheese toaster.

Cake pans, with tubes in the centre, of different shapes and sizes.
Carving knife.
Corkscrew.
Chafing dishes.
Candle stick.
Candle box.
Coffee pot.
Coffee roaster.
Canisters for coffee, tea and spices.
Coffee.
Chocolate boiler.
Cups without handles, for puffs and custards.
Coarse dish mats, to dish up on.
Coal scuttle.
Covered wooden boxes, for rice, tapioca, starch, etc.
Cheese box.
Cheese knife.
Cream whipper.
Crumb brush.
Clothes basket.
Clothes pins.
Clothes lines.
Clothes boiler.
Chopping knife.
Cleaver.
Cracker breaker.
Crocks for meat and butter
Different size bowls.
Dish covers.
Different size dishes.
Dippers.
Dish pans, for meat and butter, for washing and rinsing.
Different size jars for soda and cream of tartar.
Different size tin plates for pies.
Dust brushes.
Egg beater.
Fish knife.
Flour dredges, one for white, one for brown flour.
Flour sifter.
Fish kettle.
Faucets.
Fluid can and lamp.
Floor cloth.
Fine hair sifters of different sizes.
Frying pans for meat and butter.
Funnels.
Furniture.
Fish boards.
Fish baking pans.
Fish strainer.
Gridirons, one for fish and one for meat.
Grindstone, for sharpening knives.

Griddle.
Hammer and nails.
Ice cream freezer.
Ice blanket and box.
Iron mortar.
Iron ladle.
Iron oven, different sizes.
Iron stands.
Iron lifters.
Iron hooks.
Jelly moulds and jelly bags of flannel.
Jagging iron.
Knives and forks.
Kettles.
Knife box.
Knife for cleaning fish.
Keep in a drawer plenty of foolscap paper, twine, scissors, tape, also plenty of crash towels for meat and butter. There should also be a good supply of soap and soda; it will do the cloths good to boil them frequently in lye.
Large and small graters for horseradish and nutmeg.
Large and small iron spoon.
Larding needles that are used for inserting pieces of fat in the meat.
Lantern.
Lemon squeezers.
Lamp cleaner.
Milk.
Mop.
Meat board for chopping meat.
Mallet of wood.
Meat tongs.
Marble slab for pastry.
Marble slab for meat.
Marble slab for butter.
Meal chest and sifter.
Measures.
Mats for tables.
Muffin rings.
Mats for the feet.
Mouse trap.
Marble mortar.
Nut cracker.
Omelette frying pan.
Pudding pans.
Pastry cutter.
Paste moulds.
Pepper box.
Plate warmer.
Preserving kettles.
Porcelain stewpans to stew fish in, one for meat and one for butter.
Plane to slice dried meat.
Pudding boilers.
Pickling tubs.
Press boards, for ironing.
Potato masher.

Rolling pin for meat.
Rolling pin for butter.
Refrigerator.
Rolling pins for butter and meat.
Skimmers, perforated, for butter and meat.
Sugar sifter.
Spice sifter.
Skewers for meat and butter.
Soup kettles.
Soup ladles.
Soup strainer.
Scales and weights.
Steamer for cooking potatoes.
Smoothing irons.
Soup strainer.
Shears.
Step ladder.
Soap bowl.
Stove brush.
Starch basin.
Starch strainer.
Starch box.
Two colanders.
Two strainers for butter and meat.
Two tables and dresser.
Toasting fork.
Two towel racks, one for jack towels to wipe hands on, and the other for dish towels; all towels should have loops to be hung up.
Thermometer.
Vegetable drainer.
Vegetable boiler.
Vegetable lifters.
Wash basin.
Wooden salad spoons and forks.
Whisks of different sizes.
Waffle irons.
Wafer irons.
Wood box.
Water buckets.
Wooden bowls.
Wire covers for dishes.
Water baths for saucepans.
Wooden salad bowls.
Wash tubs.
Wash boiler.
Water pails.
Water filterer.
Water cooler.
Wedges for breaking ice.
Window brushes.
Wine cooler.

JEWISH CALENDAR.

New Moon and Feasts.

First month, *Nissan.*—1st one day (Rosh Hodesh) 13th, Eve of Passover; 14th and 15th, Passover kept in commemoration of the departure of the Israelites from Egypt and bondage. The Homer commences the 2d night of Passover and lasts 50 days; 33d day of Homer is called Lag Beomar. The middle days of Passover are 16, 17, 18, 19 of Nissan, allowed to work. The second days of the Passover are 20th and 21st of Nissan. There are 30 days in Nissan called the Lunar month; the 30th day is (Rosh Hodesh) New Moon.

Second month, *Iyar.*—1st, 2d day of (Rosh Hodesh) New Moon. 19th Lag Béomar. There are 29 days of lunar month.

Third month, *Sivan.*—1st, (Rosh Hodesh) New Moon. 5th Eve of Shebout; 6th and 7th days of Shebout, the celebration of the giving of the Commandments. There are 30 days in Sivan; the 30th day is (Rosh Hodesh) New Moon.

Fourth month, *Tamuz.*—1st, 2d day of (Rosh Hodèsh) New Moon. 17th is the Fast for the taking Jerusalem and the beginning of the three weeks of lamentation for Jerusalem. There are 29 days of lunar month.

Fifth month, *Abb.*—1st, (Rosh Hodesh) New Moon. The beginning of days of abstinence of animal food; we are commanded to fast and mourn. 9th of Abb is the Fast for the destruction of the Temple. 30th of Abb is (Rosh Hodesh) New Moon. There are 30 days in that month.

Sixth month, *Elul.*—1st, (2d Rosh Hodesh) New Moon. 29 days in that month.

Seventh month, *Tishri.*—1st and 2d, the commencement of the New Year (Rosh Hosana) and solemn feasts. There are two days, 1st and 2d; the 3d, Tishri, is the Fast of Guedaliah; the 9th is the Eve of Kippur; 10th is Kippur, or day of Atonement; 14th is the Eve of Succoth; 15th and 16th are the days of Succoth or Feast of Tabernacles. There are middle days; 17th, 18th, 19th, 20th, 21st is Hosana Raba; and the Eve of Shemence Ahzeratz; 22d and 23d are called Shemence Ahzeratz, and Sencibus Tobra, kept for celebrating the law of Moses. There are 30 days in the month of Tishri. 30th is the first day of (Rosh Hodesh) New Moon.

Eighth month, *Marchesvan.*—1st is the 2d day of (Rosh Hodesh) New Moon. There are 30 days in that month. 30th is 1st day of (Rosh Hodesh) New Moon.

Ninth month, *Kislev.*—1st is the 2d day of (Rosh Rodesh) New Moon. 25th celebrated for the consecration of the Temple, or dedication of lights in the Temple. There are 30 days in Kislev lunar month. 30th of Kislev is the 1st day of (Rosh Hodesh) New Moon.

Tenth month, *Thebet.*—1st is the 2d day of (Rosh Hodesh) New Moon. 10th is the fast for the siege of Jerusalem. There are 29 days in that month.

Eleventh month, *Shebat.*—1st (Rosh Hodesh) New Moon. There are 30 days in that month; the 30th is the first day of (Rosh Hodesh) New Moon.

Twelfth month, *Adar.*—1st, 2d day of (Rosh Hodesh) New Moon. 13th is the Fast of Esther; 14th is called Purem, commemorated for the destruction of Haman, who was hanged on the gibbet he had erected for the destruction of the Jews, who were saved by the interposition of Providence, by Mordecai the Jew and Queen Esther. There are 29 days in Adar lunar month.

Ve Adar is the 13th month in leap year, which occurs every 3d year.—1st is (Rosh Hodesh) New Moon.

A lunar year consists of 12 lunation (or months,) containing 354 days, and is 11 days shorter than the solar year, which has 365 days.

Hours for the commencement of the Sabbath.

From	January 22,	to	February 22,	at	4½	o'clock, P. M.
"	February 22,	"	March 15,	"	5	"
"	March 15,	"	April 8,	"	5½	"
"	April 8,	"	May 1,	"	6	"
"	May 1,	"	May 22,	"	6½	"
"	May 22,	"	July 22,	"	7	"
"	July 22,	"	August 22,	"	6½	"
"	August, 22,	"	September 15,	"	6	"
"	September 15,	"	October 8,	"	5½	"
"	October, 8,	"	November 1,	"	5	"
"	November 1,	"	November, 22,	"	4½	"
"	November 22,	"	January 22,	"	4	"

INDEX.

C

F

G

H

I

J

N

Q

R

S

T

A CATALOG OF SELECTED

DOVER BOOKS

IN ALL FIELDS OF INTEREST

A CATALOG OF SELECTED DOVER BOOKS IN ALL FIELDS OF INTEREST

STICKLEY CRAFTSMAN FURNITURE CATALOGS, Gustav Stickley and L. & J. G. Stickley. Beautiful, functional furniture in two authentic catalogs from 1910. 594 illustrations, including 277 photos, show settles, rockers, armchairs, reclining chairs, bookcases, desks, tables. 183pp. 6½ x 9¼. 23838-5

AMERICAN LOCOMOTIVES IN HISTORIC PHOTOGRAPHS: 1858 to 1949, Ron Ziel (ed.). A rare collection of 126 meticulously detailed official photographs, called "builder portraits," of American locomotives that majestically chronicle the rise of steam locomotive power in America. Introduction. Detailed captions. xi+ 129pp. 9 x 12. 27393-8

AMERICA'S LIGHTHOUSES: An Illustrated History, Francis Ross Holland, Jr. Delightfully written, profusely illustrated fact-filled survey of over 200 American lighthouses since 1716. History, anecdotes, technological advances, more. 240pp. 8 x 10¾. 25576-X

TOWARDS A NEW ARCHITECTURE, Le Corbusier. Pioneering manifesto by founder of "International School." Technical and aesthetic theories, views of industry, economics, relation of form to function, "mass-production split" and much more. Profusely illustrated. 320pp. 6⅛ x 9¼. (Available in U.S. only.) 25023-7

HOW THE OTHER HALF LIVES, Jacob Riis. Famous journalistic record, exposing poverty and degradation of New York slums around 1900, by major social reformer. 100 striking and influential photographs. 233pp. 10 x 7⅞. 22012-5

FRUIT KEY AND TWIG KEY TO TREES AND SHRUBS, William M. Harlow. One of the handiest and most widely used identification aids. Fruit key covers 120 deciduous and evergreen species; twig key 160 deciduous species. Easily used. Over 300 photographs. 126pp. 5⅜ x 8½. 20511-8

COMMON BIRD SONGS, Dr. Donald J. Borror. Songs of 60 most common U.S. birds: robins, sparrows, cardinals, bluejays, finches, more–arranged in order of increasing complexity. Up to 9 variations of songs of each species.
Cassette and manual 99911-4

ORCHIDS AS HOUSE PLANTS, Rebecca Tyson Northen. Grow cattleyas and many other kinds of orchids–in a window, in a case, or under artificial light. 63 illustrations. 148pp. 5⅜ x 8½. 23261-1

MONSTER MAZES, Dave Phillips. Masterful mazes at four levels of difficulty. Avoid deadly perils and evil creatures to find magical treasures. Solutions for all 32 exciting illustrated puzzles. 48pp. 8¼ x 11. 26005-4

MOZART'S DON GIOVANNI (DOVER OPERA LIBRETTO SERIES), Wolfgang Amadeus Mozart. Introduced and translated by Ellen H. Bleiler. Standard Italian libretto, with complete English translation. Convenient and thoroughly portable–an ideal companion for reading along with a recording or the performance itself. Introduction. List of characters. Plot summary. 121pp. 5¼ x 8½. 24944-1

TECHNICAL MANUAL AND DICTIONARY OF CLASSICAL BALLET, Gail Grant. Defines, explains, comments on steps, movements, poses and concepts. 15-page pictorial section. Basic book for student, viewer. 127pp. 5⅜ x 8½. 21843-0

THE CLARINET AND CLARINET PLAYING, David Pino. Lively, comprehensive work features suggestions about technique, musicianship, and musical interpretation, as well as guidelines for teaching, making your own reeds, and preparing for public performance. Includes an intriguing look at clarinet history. "A godsend," *The Clarinet,* Journal of the International Clarinet Society. Appendixes. 7 illus. 320pp. 5⅜ x 8½. 40270-3

HOLLYWOOD GLAMOR PORTRAITS, John Kobal (ed.). 145 photos from 1926-49. Harlow, Gable, Bogart, Bacall; 94 stars in all. Full background on photographers, technical aspects. 160pp. 8⅜ x 11¼. 23352-9

THE ANNOTATED CASEY AT THE BAT: A Collection of Ballads about the Mighty Casey/Third, Revised Edition, Martin Gardner (ed.). Amusing sequels and parodies of one of America's best-loved poems: Casey's Revenge, Why Casey Whiffed, Casey's Sister at the Bat, others. 256pp. 5⅜ x 8½. 28598-7

THE RAVEN AND OTHER FAVORITE POEMS, Edgar Allan Poe. Over 40 of the author's most memorable poems: "The Bells," "Ulalume," "Israfel," "To Helen," "The Conqueror Worm," "Eldorado," "Annabel Lee," many more. Alphabetic lists of titles and first lines. 64pp. 5$\frac{3}{16}$ x 8¼. 26685-0

PERSONAL MEMOIRS OF U. S. GRANT, Ulysses Simpson Grant. Intelligent, deeply moving firsthand account of Civil War campaigns, considered by many the finest military memoirs ever written. Includes letters, historic photographs, maps and more. 528pp. 6⅛ x 9¼. 28587-1

ANCIENT EGYPTIAN MATERIALS AND INDUSTRIES, A. Lucas and J. Harris. Fascinating, comprehensive, thoroughly documented text describes this ancient civilization's vast resources and the processes that incorporated them in daily life, including the use of animal products, building materials, cosmetics, perfumes and incense, fibers, glazed ware, glass and its manufacture, materials used in the mummification process, and much more. 544pp. 6⅛ x 9¼. (Available in U.S. only.) 40446-3

RUSSIAN STORIES/RUSSKIE RASSKAZY: A Dual-Language Book, edited by Gleb Struve. Twelve tales by such masters as Chekhov, Tolstoy, Dostoevsky, Pushkin, others. Excellent word-for-word English translations on facing pages, plus teaching and study aids, Russian/English vocabulary, biographical/critical introductions, more. 416pp. 5⅜ x 8½. 26244-8

PHILADELPHIA THEN AND NOW: 60 Sites Photographed in the Past and Present, Kenneth Finkel and Susan Oyama. Rare photographs of City Hall, Logan Square, Independence Hall, Betsy Ross House, other landmarks juxtaposed with contemporary views. Captures changing face of historic city. Introduction. Captions. 128pp. 8¼ x 11. 25790-8

AIA ARCHITECTURAL GUIDE TO NASSAU AND SUFFOLK COUNTIES, LONG ISLAND, The American Institute of Architects, Long Island Chapter, and the Society for the Preservation of Long Island Antiquities. Comprehensive, well-researched and generously illustrated volume brings to life over three centuries of Long Island's great architectural heritage. More than 240 photographs with authoritative, extensively detailed captions. 176pp. 8¼ x 11. 26946-9

NORTH AMERICAN INDIAN LIFE: Customs and Traditions of 23 Tribes, Elsie Clews Parsons (ed.). 27 fictionalized essays by noted anthropologists examine religion, customs, government, additional facets of life among the Winnebago, Crow, Zuni, Eskimo, other tribes. 480pp. 6⅛ x 9¼. 27377-6

FRANK LLOYD WRIGHT'S DANA HOUSE, Donald Hoffmann. Pictorial essay of residential masterpiece with over 160 interior and exterior photos, plans, elevations, sketches and studies. 128pp. 9¼ x 10¾. 29120-0

THE MALE AND FEMALE FIGURE IN MOTION: 60 Classic Photographic Sequences, Eadweard Muybridge. 60 true-action photographs of men and women walking, running, climbing, bending, turning, etc., reproduced from rare 19th-century masterpiece. vi + 121pp. 9 x 12. 24745-7

1001 QUESTIONS ANSWERED ABOUT THE SEASHORE, N. J. Berrill and Jacquelyn Berrill. Queries answered about dolphins, sea snails, sponges, starfish, fishes, shore birds, many others. Covers appearance, breeding, growth, feeding, much more. 305pp. 5¼ x 8¼. 23366-9

ATTRACTING BIRDS TO YOUR YARD, William J. Weber. Easy-to-follow guide offers advice on how to attract the greatest diversity of birds: birdhouses, feeders, water and waterers, much more. 96pp. 5$\frac{3}{16}$ x 8¼. 28927-3

MEDICINAL AND OTHER USES OF NORTH AMERICAN PLANTS: A Historical Survey with Special Reference to the Eastern Indian Tribes, Charlotte Erichsen-Brown. Chronological historical citations document 500 years of usage of plants, trees, shrubs native to eastern Canada, northeastern U.S. Also complete identifying information. 343 illustrations. 544pp. 6½ x 9¼. 25951-X

STORYBOOK MAZES, Dave Phillips. 23 stories and mazes on two-page spreads: Wizard of Oz, Treasure Island, Robin Hood, etc. Solutions. 64pp. 8¼ x 11. 23628-5

AMERICAN NEGRO SONGS: 230 Folk Songs and Spirituals, Religious and Secular, John W. Work. This authoritative study traces the African influences of songs sung and played by black Americans at work, in church, and as entertainment. The author discusses the lyric significance of such songs as "Swing Low, Sweet Chariot," "John Henry," and others and offers the words and music for 230 songs. Bibliography. Index of Song Titles. 272pp. 6½ x 9¼. 40271-1

MOVIE-STAR PORTRAITS OF THE FORTIES, John Kobal (ed.). 163 glamor, studio photos of 106 stars of the 1940s: Rita Hayworth, Ava Gardner, Marlon Brando, Clark Gable, many more. 176pp. 8⅜ x 11¼. 23546-7

BENCHLEY LOST AND FOUND, Robert Benchley. Finest humor from early 30s, about pet peeves, child psychologists, post office and others. Mostly unavailable elsewhere. 73 illustrations by Peter Arno and others. 183pp. 5⅜ x 8½. 22410-4

YEKL and THE IMPORTED BRIDEGROOM AND OTHER STORIES OF YIDDISH NEW YORK, Abraham Cahan. Film Hester Street based on *Yekl* (1896). Novel, other stories among first about Jewish immigrants on N.Y.'s East Side. 240pp. 5⅜ x 8½. 22427-9

SELECTED POEMS, Walt Whitman. Generous sampling from *Leaves of Grass*. Twenty-four poems include "I Hear America Singing," "Song of the Open Road," "I Sing the Body Electric," "When Lilacs Last in the Dooryard Bloom'd," "O Captain! My Captain!"–all reprinted from an authoritative edition. Lists of titles and first lines. 128pp. 5$\frac{3}{16}$ x 8¼. 26878-0

THE BEST TALES OF HOFFMANN, E. T. A. Hoffmann. 10 of Hoffmann's most important stories: "Nutcracker and the King of Mice," "The Golden Flowerpot," etc. 458pp. 5⅜ x 8½. 21793-0

FROM FETISH TO GOD IN ANCIENT EGYPT, E. A. Wallis Budge. Rich detailed survey of Egyptian conception of "God" and gods, magic, cult of animals, Osiris, more. Also, superb English translations of hymns and legends. 240 illustrations. 545pp. 5⅜ x 8½. 25803-3

FRENCH STORIES/CONTES FRANÇAIS: A Dual-Language Book, Wallace Fowlie. Ten stories by French masters, Voltaire to Camus: "Micromegas" by Voltaire; "The Atheist's Mass" by Balzac; "Minuet" by de Maupassant; "The Guest" by Camus, six more. Excellent English translations on facing pages. Also French-English vocabulary list, exercises, more. 352pp. 5⅜ x 8½. 26443-2

CHICAGO AT THE TURN OF THE CENTURY IN PHOTOGRAPHS: 122 Historic Views from the Collections of the Chicago Historical Society, Larry A. Viskochil. Rare large-format prints offer detailed views of City Hall, State Street, the Loop, Hull House, Union Station, many other landmarks, circa 1904-1913. Introduction. Captions. Maps. 144pp. 9⅜ x 12¼. 24656-6

OLD BROOKLYN IN EARLY PHOTOGRAPHS, 1865-1929, William Lee Younger. Luna Park, Gravesend race track, construction of Grand Army Plaza, moving of Hotel Brighton, etc. 157 previously unpublished photographs. 165pp. 8⅞ x 11¾. 23587-4

THE MYTHS OF THE NORTH AMERICAN INDIANS, Lewis Spence. Rich anthology of the myths and legends of the Algonquins, Iroquois, Pawnees and Sioux, prefaced by an extensive historical and ethnological commentary. 36 illustrations. 480pp. 5⅜ x 8½. 25967-6

AN ENCYCLOPEDIA OF BATTLES: Accounts of Over 1,560 Battles from 1479 B.C. to the Present, David Eggenberger. Essential details of every major battle in recorded history from the first battle of Megiddo in 1479 B.C. to Grenada in 1984. List of Battle Maps. New Appendix covering the years 1967-1984. Index. 99 illustrations. 544pp. 6½ x 9¼. 24913-1

SAILING ALONE AROUND THE WORLD, Captain Joshua Slocum. First man to sail around the world, alone, in small boat. One of great feats of seamanship told in delightful manner. 67 illustrations. 294pp. 5⅜ x 8½. 20326-3

ANARCHISM AND OTHER ESSAYS, Emma Goldman. Powerful, penetrating, prophetic essays on direct action, role of minorities, prison reform, puritan hypocrisy, violence, etc. 271pp. 5⅜ x 8½. 22484-8

MYTHS OF THE HINDUS AND BUDDHISTS, Ananda K. Coomaraswamy and Sister Nivedita. Great stories of the epics; deeds of Krishna, Shiva, taken from puranas, Vedas, folk tales; etc. 32 illustrations. 400pp. 5⅜ x 8½. 21759-0

THE TRAUMA OF BIRTH, Otto Rank. Rank's controversial thesis that anxiety neurosis is caused by profound psychological trauma which occurs at birth. 256pp. 5⅜ x 8½. 27974-X

A THEOLOGICO-POLITICAL TREATISE, Benedict Spinoza. Also contains unfinished Political Treatise. Great classic on religious liberty, theory of government on common consent. R. Elwes translation. Total of 421pp. 5⅜ x 8½. 20249-6

MY BONDAGE AND MY FREEDOM, Frederick Douglass. Born a slave, Douglass became outspoken force in antislavery movement. The best of Douglass' autobiographies. Graphic description of slave life. 464pp. 5⅜ x 8½. 22457-0

FOLLOWING THE EQUATOR: A Journey Around the World, Mark Twain. Fascinating humorous account of 1897 voyage to Hawaii, Australia, India, New Zealand, etc. Ironic, bemused reports on peoples, customs, climate, flora and fauna, politics, much more. 197 illustrations. 720pp. 5⅜ x 8½. 26113-1

THE PEOPLE CALLED SHAKERS, Edward D. Andrews. Definitive study of Shakers: origins, beliefs, practices, dances, social organization, furniture and crafts, etc. 33 illustrations. 351pp. 5⅜ x 8½. 21081-2

THE MYTHS OF GREECE AND ROME, H. A. Guerber. A classic of mythology, generously illustrated, long prized for its simple, graphic, accurate retelling of the principal myths of Greece and Rome, and for its commentary on their origins and significance. With 64 illustrations by Michelangelo, Raphael, Titian, Rubens, Canova, Bernini and others. 480pp. 5⅜ x 8½. 27584-1

PSYCHOLOGY OF MUSIC, Carl E. Seashore. Classic work discusses music as a medium from psychological viewpoint. Clear treatment of physical acoustics, auditory apparatus, sound perception, development of musical skills, nature of musical feeling, host of other topics. 88 figures. 408pp. 5⅜ x 8½. 21851-1

THE PHILOSOPHY OF HISTORY, Georg W. Hegel. Great classic of Western thought develops concept that history is not chance but rational process, the evolution of freedom. 457pp. 5⅜ x 8½. 20112-0

THE BOOK OF TEA, Kakuzo Okakura. Minor classic of the Orient: entertaining, charming explanation, interpretation of traditional Japanese culture in terms of tea ceremony. 94pp. 5⅜ x 8½. 20070-1

LIFE IN ANCIENT EGYPT, Adolf Erman. Fullest, most thorough, detailed older account with much not in more recent books, domestic life, religion, magic, medicine, commerce, much more. Many illustrations reproduce tomb paintings, carvings, hieroglyphs, etc. 597pp. 5⅜ x 8½. 22632-8

SUNDIALS, Their Theory and Construction, Albert Waugh. Far and away the best, most thorough coverage of ideas, mathematics concerned, types, construction, adjusting anywhere. Simple, nontechnical treatment allows even children to build several of these dials. Over 100 illustrations. 230pp. 5⅜ x 8½. 22947-5

THEORETICAL HYDRODYNAMICS, L. M. Milne-Thomson. Classic exposition of the mathematical theory of fluid motion, applicable to both hydrodynamics and aerodynamics. Over 600 exercises. 768pp. 6⅛ x 9¼. 68970-0

SONGS OF EXPERIENCE: Facsimile Reproduction with 26 Plates in Full Color, William Blake. 26 full-color plates from a rare 1826 edition. Includes "The Tyger," "London," "Holy Thursday," and other poems. Printed text of poems. 48pp. 5¼ x 7. 24636-1

OLD-TIME VIGNETTES IN FULL COLOR, Carol Belanger Grafton (ed.). Over 390 charming, often sentimental illustrations, selected from archives of Victorian graphics–pretty women posing, children playing, food, flowers, kittens and puppies, smiling cherubs, birds and butterflies, much more. All copyright-free. 48pp. 9¼ x 12¼. 27269-9

PERSPECTIVE FOR ARTISTS, Rex Vicat Cole. Depth, perspective of sky and sea, shadows, much more, not usually covered. 391 diagrams, 81 reproductions of drawings and paintings. 279pp. 5⅜ x 8½. 22487-2

DRAWING THE LIVING FIGURE, Joseph Sheppard. Innovative approach to artistic anatomy focuses on specifics of surface anatomy, rather than muscles and bones. Over 170 drawings of live models in front, back and side views, and in widely varying poses. Accompanying diagrams. 177 illustrations. Introduction. Index. 144pp. 8⅜ x11¼. 26723-7

GOTHIC AND OLD ENGLISH ALPHABETS: 100 Complete Fonts, Dan X. Solo. Add power, elegance to posters, signs, other graphics with 100 stunning copyright-free alphabets: Blackstone, Dolbey, Germania, 97 more–including many lower-case, numerals, punctuation marks. 104pp. 8⅛ x 11. 24695-7

HOW TO DO BEADWORK, Mary White. Fundamental book on craft from simple projects to five-bead chains and woven works. 106 illustrations. 142pp. 5⅜ x 8. 20697-1

THE BOOK OF WOOD CARVING, Charles Marshall Sayers. Finest book for beginners discusses fundamentals and offers 34 designs. "Absolutely first rate . . . well thought out and well executed."–E. J. Tangerman. 118pp. 7¾ x 10⅝. 23654-4

ILLUSTRATED CATALOG OF CIVIL WAR MILITARY GOODS: Union Army Weapons, Insignia, Uniform Accessories, and Other Equipment, Schuyler, Hartley, and Graham. Rare, profusely illustrated 1846 catalog includes Union Army uniform and dress regulations, arms and ammunition, coats, insignia, flags, swords, rifles, etc. 226 illustrations. 160pp. 9 x 12. 24939-5

WOMEN'S FASHIONS OF THE EARLY 1900s: An Unabridged Republication of "New York Fashions, 1909," National Cloak & Suit Co. Rare catalog of mail-order fashions documents women's and children's clothing styles shortly after the turn of the century. Captions offer full descriptions, prices. Invaluable resource for fashion, costume historians. Approximately 725 illustrations. 128pp. 8⅜ x 11¼. 27276-1

THE 1912 AND 1915 GUSTAV STICKLEY FURNITURE CATALOGS, Gustav Stickley. With over 200 detailed illustrations and descriptions, these two catalogs are essential reading and reference materials and identification guides for Stickley furniture. Captions cite materials, dimensions and prices. 112pp. 6½ x 9¼. 26676-1

EARLY AMERICAN LOCOMOTIVES, John H. White, Jr. Finest locomotive engravings from early 19th century: historical (1804–74), main-line (after 1870), special, foreign, etc. 147 plates. 142pp. 11⅜ x 8¼. 22772-3

THE TALL SHIPS OF TODAY IN PHOTOGRAPHS, Frank O. Braynard. Lavishly illustrated tribute to nearly 100 majestic contemporary sailing vessels: Amerigo Vespucci, Clearwater, Constitution, Eagle, Mayflower, Sea Cloud, Victory, many more. Authoritative captions provide statistics, background on each ship. 190 black-and-white photographs and illustrations. Introduction. 128pp. 8⅞ x 11¾. 27163-3

LITTLE BOOK OF EARLY AMERICAN CRAFTS AND TRADES, Peter Stockham (ed.). 1807 children's book explains crafts and trades: baker, hatter, cooper, potter, and many others. 23 copperplate illustrations. 140pp. $4\frac{5}{8}$ x 6. 23336-7

VICTORIAN FASHIONS AND COSTUMES FROM HARPER'S BAZAR, 1867–1898, Stella Blum (ed.). Day costumes, evening wear, sports clothes, shoes, hats, other accessories in over 1,000 detailed engravings. 320pp. $9\frac{3}{8}$ x $12\frac{1}{4}$. 22990-4

GUSTAV STICKLEY, THE CRAFTSMAN, Mary Ann Smith. Superb study surveys broad scope of Stickley's achievement, especially in architecture. Design philosophy, rise and fall of the Craftsman empire, descriptions and floor plans for many Craftsman houses, more. 86 black-and-white halftones. 31 line illustrations. Introduction 208pp. $6\frac{1}{2}$ x $9\frac{1}{4}$. 27210-9

THE LONG ISLAND RAIL ROAD IN EARLY PHOTOGRAPHS, Ron Ziel. Over 220 rare photos, informative text document origin (1844) and development of rail service on Long Island. Vintage views of early trains, locomotives, stations, passengers, crews, much more. Captions. $8\frac{7}{8}$ x $11\frac{3}{4}$. 26301-0

VOYAGE OF THE LIBERDADE, Joshua Slocum. Great 19th-century mariner's thrilling, first-hand account of the wreck of his ship off South America, the 35-foot boat he built from the wreckage, and its remarkable voyage home. 128pp. $5\frac{3}{8}$ x $8\frac{1}{2}$. 40022-0

TEN BOOKS ON ARCHITECTURE, Vitruvius. The most important book ever written on architecture. Early Roman aesthetics, technology, classical orders, site selection, all other aspects. Morgan translation. 331pp. $5\frac{3}{8}$ x $8\frac{1}{2}$. 20645-9

THE HUMAN FIGURE IN MOTION, Eadweard Muybridge. More than 4,500 stopped-action photos, in action series, showing undraped men, women, children jumping, lying down, throwing, sitting, wrestling, carrying, etc. 390pp. $7\frac{7}{8}$ x $10\frac{5}{8}$. 20204-6 Clothbd.

TREES OF THE EASTERN AND CENTRAL UNITED STATES AND CANADA, William M. Harlow. Best one-volume guide to 140 trees. Full descriptions, woodlore, range, etc. Over 600 illustrations. Handy size. 288pp. $4\frac{1}{2}$ x $6\frac{3}{8}$. 20395-6

SONGS OF WESTERN BIRDS, Dr. Donald J. Borror. Complete song and call repertoire of 60 western species, including flycatchers, juncoes, cactus wrens, many more–includes fully illustrated booklet. Cassette and manual 99913-0

GROWING AND USING HERBS AND SPICES, Milo Miloradovich. Versatile handbook provides all the information needed for cultivation and use of all the herbs and spices available in North America. 4 illustrations. Index. Glossary. 236pp. $5\frac{3}{8}$ x $8\frac{1}{2}$. 25058-X

BIG BOOK OF MAZES AND LABYRINTHS, Walter Shepherd. 50 mazes and labyrinths in all–classical, solid, ripple, and more–in one great volume. Perfect inexpensive puzzler for clever youngsters. Full solutions. 112pp. $8\frac{1}{8}$ x 11. 22951-3

PIANO TUNING, J. Cree Fischer. Clearest, best book for beginner, amateur. Simple repairs, raising dropped notes, tuning by easy method of flattened fifths. No previous skills needed. 4 illustrations. 201pp. 5⅜ x 8½. 23267-0

HINTS TO SINGERS, Lillian Nordica. Selecting the right teacher, developing confidence, overcoming stage fright, and many other important skills receive thoughtful discussion in this indispensible guide, written by a world-famous diva of four decades' experience. 96pp. 5⅜ x 8½. 40094-8

THE COMPLETE NONSENSE OF EDWARD LEAR, Edward Lear. All nonsense limericks, zany alphabets, Owl and Pussycat, songs, nonsense botany, etc., illustrated by Lear. Total of 320pp. 5⅜ x 8½. (Available in U.S. only.) 20167-8

VICTORIAN PARLOUR POETRY: An Annotated Anthology, Michael R. Turner. 117 gems by Longfellow, Tennyson, Browning, many lesser-known poets. "The Village Blacksmith," "Curfew Must Not Ring Tonight," "Only a Baby Small," dozens more, often difficult to find elsewhere. Index of poets, titles, first lines. xxiii + 325pp. 5⅝ x 8¼. 27044-0

DUBLINERS, James Joyce. Fifteen stories offer vivid, tightly focused observations of the lives of Dublin's poorer classes. At least one, "The Dead," is considered a masterpiece. Reprinted complete and unabridged from standard edition. 160pp. 5$\frac{3}{16}$ x 8¼. 26870-5

GREAT WEIRD TALES: 14 Stories by Lovecraft, Blackwood, Machen and Others, S. T. Joshi (ed.). 14 spellbinding tales, including "The Sin Eater," by Fiona McLeod, "The Eye Above the Mantel," by Frank Belknap Long, as well as renowned works by R. H. Barlow, Lord Dunsany, Arthur Machen, W. C. Morrow and eight other masters of the genre. 256pp. 5⅜ x 8½. (Available in U.S. only.) 40436-6

THE BOOK OF THE SACRED MAGIC OF ABRAMELIN THE MAGE, translated by S. MacGregor Mathers. Medieval manuscript of ceremonial magic. Basic document in Aleister Crowley, Golden Dawn groups. 268pp. 5⅜ x 8½. 23211-5

NEW RUSSIAN-ENGLISH AND ENGLISH-RUSSIAN DICTIONARY, M. A. O'Brien. This is a remarkably handy Russian dictionary, containing a surprising amount of information, including over 70,000 entries. 366pp. 4½ x 6⅛. 20208-9

HISTORIC HOMES OF THE AMERICAN PRESIDENTS, Second, Revised Edition, Irvin Haas. A traveler's guide to American Presidential homes, most open to the public, depicting and describing homes occupied by every American President from George Washington to George Bush. With visiting hours, admission charges, travel routes. 175 photographs. Index. 160pp. 8¼ x 11. 26751-2

NEW YORK IN THE FORTIES, Andreas Feininger. 162 brilliant photographs by the well-known photographer, formerly with *Life* magazine. Commuters, shoppers, Times Square at night, much else from city at its peak. Captions by John von Hartz. 181pp. 9¼ x 10¾. 23585-8

INDIAN SIGN LANGUAGE, William Tomkins. Over 525 signs developed by Sioux and other tribes. Written instructions and diagrams. Also 290 pictographs. 111pp. 6⅛ x 9¼. 22029-X

PHOTOGRAPHIC SKETCHBOOK OF THE CIVIL WAR, Alexander Gardner. 100 photos taken on field during the Civil War. Famous shots of Manassas Harper's Ferry, Lincoln, Richmond, slave pens, etc. 244pp. 10⅝ x 8¼. 22731-6

FIVE ACRES AND INDEPENDENCE, Maurice G. Kains. Great back-to-the-land classic explains basics of self-sufficient farming. The one book to get. 95 illustrations. 397pp. 5⅜ x 8½. 20974-1

SONGS OF EASTERN BIRDS, Dr. Donald J. Borror. Songs and calls of 60 species most common to eastern U.S.: warblers, woodpeckers, flycatchers, thrushes, larks, many more in high-quality recording. Cassette and manual 99912-2

A MODERN HERBAL, Margaret Grieve. Much the fullest, most exact, most useful compilation of herbal material. Gigantic alphabetical encyclopedia, from aconite to zedoary, gives botanical information, medical properties, folklore, economic uses, much else. Indispensable to serious reader. 161 illustrations. 888pp. 6½ x 9¼. 2-vol. set. (Available in U.S. only.) Vol. I: 22798-7
Vol. II: 22799-5

HIDDEN TREASURE MAZE BOOK, Dave Phillips. Solve 34 challenging mazes accompanied by heroic tales of adventure. Evil dragons, people-eating plants, blood-thirsty giants, many more dangerous adversaries lurk at every twist and turn. 34 mazes, stories, solutions. 48pp. 8¼ x 11. 24566-7

LETTERS OF W. A. MOZART, Wolfgang A. Mozart. Remarkable letters show bawdy wit, humor, imagination, musical insights, contemporary musical world; includes some letters from Leopold Mozart. 276pp. 5⅜ x 8½. 22859-2

BASIC PRINCIPLES OF CLASSICAL BALLET, Agrippina Vaganova. Great Russian theoretician, teacher explains methods for teaching classical ballet. 118 illustrations. 175pp. 5⅜ x 8½. 22036-2

THE JUMPING FROG, Mark Twain. Revenge edition. The original story of The Celebrated Jumping Frog of Calaveras County, a hapless French translation, and Twain's hilarious "retranslation" from the French. 12 illustrations. 66pp. 5⅜ x 8½. 22686-7

BEST REMEMBERED POEMS, Martin Gardner (ed.). The 126 poems in this superb collection of 19th- and 20th-century British and American verse range from Shelley's "To a Skylark" to the impassioned "Renascence" of Edna St. Vincent Millay and to Edward Lear's whimsical "The Owl and the Pussycat." 224pp. 5⅜ x 8½. 27165-X

COMPLETE SONNETS, William Shakespeare. Over 150 exquisite poems deal with love, friendship, the tyranny of time, beauty's evanescence, death and other themes in language of remarkable power, precision and beauty. Glossary of archaic terms. 80pp. $5\frac{3}{16}$ x 8¼. 26686-9

THE BATTLES THAT CHANGED HISTORY, Fletcher Pratt. Eminent historian profiles 16 crucial conflicts, ancient to modern, that changed the course of civilization. 352pp. 5⅜ x 8½. 41129-X

THE WIT AND HUMOR OF OSCAR WILDE, Alvin Redman (ed.). More than 1,000 ripostes, paradoxes, wisecracks: Work is the curse of the drinking classes; I can resist everything except temptation; etc. 258pp. 5⅜ x 8½. 20602-5

SHAKESPEARE LEXICON AND QUOTATION DICTIONARY, Alexander Schmidt. Full definitions, locations, shades of meaning in every word in plays and poems. More than 50,000 exact quotations. 1,485pp. 6½ x 9¼. 2-vol. set.
Vol. 1: 22726-X
Vol. 2: 22727-8

SELECTED POEMS, Emily Dickinson. Over 100 best-known, best-loved poems by one of America's foremost poets, reprinted from authoritative early editions. No comparable edition at this price. Index of first lines. 64pp. 5³⁄₁₆ x 8¼. 26466-1

THE INSIDIOUS DR. FU-MANCHU, Sax Rohmer. The first of the popular mystery series introduces a pair of English detectives to their archnemesis, the diabolical Dr. Fu-Manchu. Flavorful atmosphere, fast-paced action, and colorful characters enliven this classic of the genre. 208pp. 5³⁄₁₆ x 8¼. 29898-1

THE MALLEUS MALEFICARUM OF KRAMER AND SPRENGER, translated by Montague Summers. Full text of most important witchhunter's "bible," used by both Catholics and Protestants. 278pp. 6⅝ x 10. 22802-9

SPANISH STORIES/CUENTOS ESPAÑOLES: A Dual-Language Book, Angel Flores (ed.). Unique format offers 13 great stories in Spanish by Cervantes, Borges, others. Faithful English translations on facing pages. 352pp. 5⅜ x 8½. 25399-6

GARDEN CITY, LONG ISLAND, IN EARLY PHOTOGRAPHS, 1869–1919, Mildred H. Smith. Handsome treasury of 118 vintage pictures, accompanied by carefully researched captions, document the Garden City Hotel fire (1899), the Vanderbilt Cup Race (1908), the first airmail flight departing from the Nassau Boulevard Aerodrome (1911), and much more. 96pp. 8⅞ x 11¾. 40669-5

OLD QUEENS, N.Y., IN EARLY PHOTOGRAPHS, Vincent F. Seyfried and William Asadorian. Over 160 rare photographs of Maspeth, Jamaica, Jackson Heights, and other areas. Vintage views of DeWitt Clinton mansion, 1939 World's Fair and more. Captions. 192pp. 8⅞ x 11. 26358-4

CAPTURED BY THE INDIANS: 15 Firsthand Accounts, 1750-1870, Frederick Drimmer. Astounding true historical accounts of grisly torture, bloody conflicts, relentless pursuits, miraculous escapes and more, by people who lived to tell the tale. 384pp. 5⅜ x 8½. 24901-8

THE WORLD'S GREAT SPEECHES (Fourth Enlarged Edition), Lewis Copeland, Lawrence W. Lamm, and Stephen J. McKenna. Nearly 300 speeches provide public speakers with a wealth of updated quotes and inspiration–from Pericles' funeral oration and William Jennings Bryan's "Cross of Gold Speech" to Malcolm X's powerful words on the Black Revolution and Earl of Spenser's tribute to his sister, Diana, Princess of Wales. 944pp. 5⅜ x 8⅜. 40903-1

THE BOOK OF THE SWORD, Sir Richard F. Burton. Great Victorian scholar/adventurer's eloquent, erudite history of the "queen of weapons"–from prehistory to early Roman Empire. Evolution and development of early swords, variations (sabre, broadsword, cutlass, scimitar, etc.), much more. 336pp. 6⅛ x 9¼. 25434-8

CATALOG OF DOVER BOOKS

THE STORY OF THE TITANIC AS TOLD BY ITS SURVIVORS, Jack Winocour (ed.). What it was really like. Panic, despair, shocking inefficiency, and a little heroism. More thrilling than any fictional account. 26 illustrations. 320pp. 5⅜ x 8½. 20610-6

FAIRY AND FOLK TALES OF THE IRISH PEASANTRY, William Butler Yeats (ed.). Treasury of 64 tales from the twilight world of Celtic myth and legend: "The Soul Cages," "The Kildare Pooka," "King O'Toole and his Goose," many more. Introduction and Notes by W. B. Yeats. 352pp. 5⅜ x 8½. 26941-8

BUDDHIST MAHAYANA TEXTS, E. B. Cowell and others (eds.). Superb, accurate translations of basic documents in Mahayana Buddhism, highly important in history of religions. The Buddha-karita of Asvaghosha, Larger Sukhavativyuha, more. 448pp. 5⅜ x 8½. 25552-2

ONE TWO THREE . . . INFINITY: Facts and Speculations of Science, George Gamow. Great physicist's fascinating, readable overview of contemporary science: number theory, relativity, fourth dimension, entropy, genes, atomic structure, much more. 128 illustrations. Index. 352pp. 5⅜ x 8½. 25664-2

EXPERIMENTATION AND MEASUREMENT, W. J. Youden. Introductory manual explains laws of measurement in simple terms and offers tips for achieving accuracy and minimizing errors. Mathematics of measurement, use of instruments, experimenting with machines. 1994 edition. Foreword. Preface. Introduction. Epilogue. Selected Readings. Glossary. Index. Tables and figures. 128pp. 5⅜ x 8½. 40451-X

DALÍ ON MODERN ART: The Cuckolds of Antiquated Modern Art, Salvador Dalí. Influential painter skewers modern art and its practitioners. Outrageous evaluations of Picasso, Cézanne, Turner, more. 15 renderings of paintings discussed. 44 calligraphic decorations by Dalí. 96pp. 5⅜ x 8½. (Available in U.S. only.) 29220-7

ANTIQUE PLAYING CARDS: A Pictorial History, Henry René D'Allemagne. Over 900 elaborate, decorative images from rare playing cards (14th–20th centuries): Bacchus, death, dancing dogs, hunting scenes, royal coats of arms, players cheating, much more. 96pp. 9¼ x 12¼. 29265-7

MAKING FURNITURE MASTERPIECES: 30 Projects with Measured Drawings, Franklin H. Gottshall. Step-by-step instructions, illustrations for constructing handsome, useful pieces, among them a Sheraton desk, Chippendale chair, Spanish desk, Queen Anne table and a William and Mary dressing mirror. 224pp. 8⅛ x 11¼. 29338-6

THE FOSSIL BOOK: A Record of Prehistoric Life, Patricia V. Rich et al. Profusely illustrated definitive guide covers everything from single-celled organisms and dinosaurs to birds and mammals and the interplay between climate and man. Over 1,500 illustrations. 760pp. 7½ x 10⅛. 29371-8

Paperbound unless otherwise indicated. Available at your book dealer, online at **www.doverpublications.com**, or by writing to Dept. GI, Dover Publications, Inc., 31 East 2nd Street, Mineola, NY 11501. For current price information or for free catalogues (please indicate field of interest), write to Dover Publications or log on to **www.doverpublications.com** and see every Dover book in print. Dover publishes more than 500 books each year on science, elementary and advanced mathematics, biology, music, art, literary history, social sciences, and other areas.